The House at Capo d'Orso

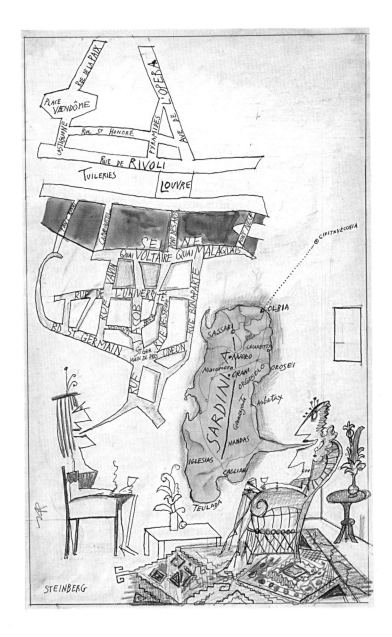

Saul Steinberg, *Untitled* (Paris/Sardinia), 1963.
© The Art Institute of Chicago/Art Resource, NY/Scala, Florence.

The House at Capo d'Orso

Sebastiano Brandolini

THE MIT PRESS
Cambridge, Massachusetts . London, England

Life lies before us, as a huge quarry lies before the architect: he deserves not the name of architect, except when, out of this fortuitous mass, he can combine, with the greatest economy and fitness and durability, some form, the pattern of which originated in his spirit.

—J. W. v. Goethe,
Wilhelm Meister's Apprenticeship and Travels, 1796

Preface 9

I wrote this book in Milan during the COVID-19 pandemic, between 2020 and 2021. The various lockdowns of the city, accompanied by the sound of endless ambulances passing through the streets with their sirens blaring, helped me to find the desire, the time, and the concentration necessary to embark on this project of self-reflection, although it is one which I had already started to think about before. For the final revision I isolated myself for a couple of weeks in the house at Palau that is the subject of this book; and it could not have been otherwise. Someone once said that this house would be the perfect place to escape to in the tragic eventuality of a pandemic. It is a house capable of creating a parallel reality, like the one in which Giovanni Boccaccio had the party of young people take refuge from the Black Death and while away the time by telling each other the hundred tales of the *Decameron* amidst much laughter and carousing.

The book is faithful to my reminiscences. Some, precisely because they are now faded and vague, have perhaps gained in fascination and significance for this very reason. With a bit of imagination, I've been able to work out how some things might have gone if they'd actually happened. To write I drew on my memory too, even though at times it took imagination for me to be able to remember. For me, knowledge, awareness, and imagination are three different versions of the same thing, thought.

In addition to explaining how the house was conceived and built, in this book I've set out above all to describe what the house has conveyed and taught to those who have been there and got to know it. The protagonist of this book is the house, not its inhabitants. I think that good architecture is also a good teacher, just like a good book, a beautiful picture, or a journey. We are all shaped and educated by the places in which we pass our lives; places settle in our minds, resurfacing at times but most of the time left to sleep; this does not mean that they disappear. This house has taught many to let the hours of the day slip by, to watch, and to listen, to sharpen the senses and feel free. While writing this book, there were moments when I had to call a halt to the flow of events that continued to spring to mind, feeling overwhelmed. There are few houses—I believe—capable of producing so many stimuli and associations. It is not an ordinary house like the ones that can be found in so many nondescript and uninteresting places in the world. It is in a precise location, was built for a specific purpose, and can be traced back to a given moment in the life of my parents and the geography of our country. It lacks the kind of half-measures with which one might disagree. It's a house that takes hold of you and doesn't let go; it is loyal and demands respect; if you offend it you're going to know about it; even though it's robust, it needs to be treated with delicacy. When it's empty it waits for you patiently, but when it's occupied it participates fully in all the activities that go on inside it. It hides nothing and reveals all. In the end, there is even something tragic about its nudity, something difficult to express.

Schematically, the chapters are divided into three groups: there are the more autobiographical ones, the ones that speak mostly of architecture, and the ones that focus more on the landscape. They shade into and overlap with one another to get across the idea that the house is not the fruit of rational logic, but of a procedure that I would define as ambiguous and unsettled. My parents, in conceiving, building, and using it, took an approach that was at once deductive and inductive, passing freely from the universal to the particular and from the particular to the universal. For them, their lifestyle, and the place they lived were one and the same thing. Trusting their instincts, they didn't worry too much about whether their decisions were reasonable.

The people mentioned in the book are all real, even when I don't give their names. Over the years there have been many who have spent time at the house, people of different ages, professions, and sorts. Some arrived there by boat, staying just long enough for a quick glass of *vernaccia* on the rocks; others have remained for a long time, bringing their cars with them; some have come on foot or by motorbike. Without being aware of it, each of them has contributed to the aura of mystery that still surrounds it today, and that leads people to talk about it as if it were a private myth. It's certainly not the kind of house that needs a guest book in which visitors sign their names. I have vivid memories of the home help from the Veneto who followed us on the adventure of the house in the very early years, especially Maria and Bruna; for them going to Sardinia was a great journey. For years our local factotum was Gino, who fished for us, transported things, and repaired them and sorted out the various pickles that we incompetent Milanese got ourselves into; every so often he slept in the living room and he even went around with a pistol in his pocket. Many friends hold this house dear and talk about it with feeling. My ex-wife Chiara loved it a lot and I hope she has good memories of it; our son Martino, very attached to the place ever since he spent his first summer vacations here with his grandparents, longs for it from faraway London where he lives.

The fact that this is a hybrid and hesitant book has meant that I have tried the patience of many friends, asking them what they thought of it and whether my private affairs could really be of any interest. Among them: Enrico Arosio, Agata Bazzi, Rita Capezzuto, Alfonso Cendron, Pietro Crepax, Gianni De Murtas, Louisa Hutton, Antonio Longo, Tommaso Marmo, Pepi Vagge, Brendan Woods and Marco Zanuso.

I will be forever grateful to Thomas Weaver of the MIT Press, with whom I've shared the idea and the gestation of the book from the outset, for his inputs from the viewpoint of its conception, publishing and writing. The fact that for both of us books are solid objects printed on paper that need to be carefully considered and constructed, just like houses built of brick and stone, has strengthened our mutual understanding. Your belief in it, Tom, has allowed me to believe in it too.

I am also hugely grateful to Huw (Shanti) Evans for his fine translation, to Sarah Handelman for her sensitive copy-edit, and to Luca Casonato for the wonderful set of photographs he made of the house and its surroundings, and which appear within this book as their own autonomous inserts.

But at the end of it all, I dedicate this book to Alba, who has always fought and continues to fight with indomitable energy to ensure that the basic simplicity of the house at Palau is preserved and looked after, day by day, without shortcuts or vacillations.

Every house is a tangled web of things and incidents, a strange conjuncture that often seems to turn into a conspiracy. It is three things at once: the autobiography of whoever has built and used it, a portrait of the place it occupies, and the chance product of a range of temporal factors that may not germinate for years after they are encountered. Each house is associated with people, with geography, and with history. This is a book of architecture that describes the web that time has woven around a particular vacation home, and one whose eccentricities continue to evolve and reveal new facets. The house is not my own work, but that of my parents; to them must go the credit for having conceived and created it. I inherited the place and today I am just the beneficiary and caretaker. My name may appear in the land register, but sentimentally it belongs to all those who, having spent time there, have enjoyed, understood, and even loved it, experiences which are possible only in this order. The house is located at Porto Ulisse, near Capo d'Orso, in the municipality of Palau, in the region of Gallura, on the island of Sardinia, in Italy, in the Mediterranean. It carries no postal address. A lot of people have slept or eaten there, but only a few have absorbed its essence.

Usually, those who do seem to understand the essence of the house begin to behave a little strangely, as if they were under its spell. They start to lose the power of speech, their movements slow down, they no longer respect the habits of fixed times, they avoid eating certain things, their gaze is frequently caught and held for long periods of time, their senses of hearing and smell are sharpened, they have absurd reactions, and present unexpected points of view, ideas that are revolutionary and anarchic. They raise fundamental questions about their lives, and in assigning less importance to practical matters lay themselves open to mystical notions or considerations of a religious order. These are just some of the possible side effects of the architecture and the place, which can vary widely.

When someone dies or goes away, houses are among the first things to change, and often to melt away and vanish. The furniture and other objects are discarded or divided among the heirs or put up for auction, or they change their position and their significance; papers that were thought to still be there disappear and have to be searched for; things which were thought to have been lost forever turn up unexpectedly, and in the end, in one way or another, everything is different. A new taste and a new approach to living arrive with the new owners or inhabitants; furniture stores change with every generation, and people's homes take on a wholly different flavor. Newcomers usually make small but significant modifications, and thereby leave their individual marks; houses often turn into pastiches, and it is rare for the atmosphere and lifestyle of places as they were when they were born to be preserved. Even though the thorough iconographic and factual research carried out for historical movies and TV series helps us to understand and imagine what the houses of Pompeii, Venetian palazzi, Victorian country houses, or the Forbidden City in Beijing were once like, we are left with the impression that as generations succeed one another the original atmosphere of the architecture is always lost, and hardly ever replaced by something equally coherent and poetic. Perhaps atmosphere, so ephemeral and ethereal, is the true substance of architecture.

This sense of the effective impossibility of *really* preserving the spirit of a house was something I felt strongly in Nuoro, the city at the heart of Sardinia, when I visited the house-museum of Grazia Deledda (1871–1936), winner of the Nobel Prize in Literature in 1926. The house dates from the second half of the nineteenth century and is located in Santu Pedru, a district inhabited by shepherds in the oldest part of the city. It is an example of a well-to-do Nuorese residence, on three stories, and with several inner courtyards on the ground floor: solid, well organized, and harmoniously proportioned. Deledda lived there until her marriage in 1900, when she moved to Rome. In 1913 the house was sold, but not subjected to alterations; later it was declared a national monument and in 1968 it was purchased by the municipality of Nuoro, which in 1979 handed it over to the ISRE (Istituto Superiore Regionale Etnografico) for the symbolic price of 1,000 lire. Over the years the institute, gradually coming into possession of manuscripts, photographs, documents, furniture, and personal items belonging to the writer, turned it into a house-museum, complete with many of the things that go into making a home. The kitchen is equipped with pans and baking molds; the room once used for carding and weaving wool has been put in order; the papers and books in the study are carefully arranged; the implements used for sheep-farming in the shady walled garden look ready for use. It is even explained to the visitor how the house was heated a hundred years ago (with an ingenious system of basins filled with burning coals), given that Nuoro is in the mountains and very cold in the winter. But as in all house-museums, and notwithstanding the faithful and painstaking historical reconstruction, what is missing here is the essence of what we might call the atmosphere of the great writer's private world, at once evanescent and substantial. Was the house *really* like that? You come away with the impression that this is an excellent replica, but still a replica. The furniture and the knickknacks are there, but the spirit, the people, the sounds, the smells are lacking. Nothing is out of place; the pots and baskets have been emptied, literally and metaphorically. And so we realize just how difficult it is, however hard we try, to replicate the web of things and incidents that renders every house unique. Perhaps the best way to describe a place as it really was is in writing. Grazia Deledda's last but unfinished work, *Cosima*, is an autobiography in which the descriptions of the family home in Santu Pedru are concrete and atmospheric, more faithful than its material reconstruction. *Cosima* is a book of architecture, even though there are no images. Indeed, perhaps for this very reason, I cannot help but quote a passage from this book.

> The house was simple, but comfortable: two large rooms on each floor, with low ceilings, wooden floors and whitewashed walls; the entrance was divided in two by a partition: on the right the stairs, the first flight of granite, the rest of slate; on the left a few steps leading down to the cellar. ... The room to the left of the entrance furnished with a high hard bed, a desk, a wide walnut wardrobe, and straw-bottomed, rustic-looking chairs gaily painted a light blue, was adapted to many uses; the room on the right was the dining room with a chestnut table, chairs like those others, and a fireplace with a beaten earth floor. Nothing else. Another entrance with a solid door also locked by hooks and chains led to the kitchen. And the kitchen was, as in all houses still patriarchal, the room most lived in, most warm with life and intimacy. ... All in all, everything was simple and old in the ample kitchen well illuminated by a window that looked out onto the kitchen garden, and by a glass pane in the door leading to the courtyard. In the corner near the window, rose the massive oven with its smoke pipe in the wall and three burners along the edge; in a brazier next to these there was kept, night and day lit and covered with ashes, a bit of coke, and under the stone sink beneath the window, there was a bit of coal in a small cork bucket. But most often the meals were cooked over the flames of the fireplace or of the hearth, on thick tripods that could have served as seats. All the household furnishings in the kitchen were big and solid: the carefully plated bronze frying pans, the low chairs around the fireplace, the stools, the shelves for the crockery, the marble mortar to crush the salt, the table

and the sideboard on which besides the pots was a wooden receptacle full of grated cheese, and for the servants a basket full of barley bread and something to munch with it.

According to this lengthy description a house can be summed up in the objects it contains, and these give a meaning to the way in which we live. Certain household articles reify our experiences and end up as self-portraits; others, originally practical objects, come to play an emotional role as well. The Museo del Costume in Nuoro displays Sardinian artifacts that are both decorative and useful, making us realize just how difficult it is to separate the two aspects. Jasper Morrison has published a whole book on the everyday objects of Portugal. Grazia Deledda, in her clean and objective style, describes the geography of the items in her house so well that she is able to make their utility tally with the empathy she felt toward them as a girl.

There are times when I am surprised by just how little trouble the history of architecture has taken to describe and re-create the atmosphere and light that once emanated and still emanates today from the places, buildings, facades, houses, rooms, materials, and finishes of the past. Even today's architectural criticism takes little account of the atmosphere of places and glosses over this aspect, perhaps because it is considered too subjective, even too intimate, for it to be tackled with due objectivity. The history of architecture prefers to devote itself to describing in great detail the more concrete and perhaps more banal aspects of buildings, such as their form, organization, structure, language, and style. The widespread reification of domestic architecture today constitutes a problem, one that is far from secondary and, paradoxically, fostered by the interior design magazines, which perpetuate the idea of the discipline as a separate branch of architecture rather than an essential component of its identity.

One of the themes of this book is tourism, and its role in the formation of new urban settlements, new landscapes, and a new collective imagination. In my view the architecture of tourism comprises all vacation homes, hotels, and activities ancillary to the fundamental economy, be they in the city, at the seaside, in the mountains, or in the countryside. Villages, towns, and cities where the majority of the accommodation is connected with tourism should be regarded as resorts. In short, tourism has become the raison d'être of many places. From this perspective, my house, and Palau, are in every respect part of the phenomenon of tourism. In Sardinia, I am a tourist who observes the situation from the outside and is concerned principally with what pertains to him; here I am a visitor and have never become a resident. The people of Palau see the tourist resorts as something that does not concern them personally and for which they have only indirect responsibility. The tourists' Palau is ten times bigger than the residents' Palau. So I wonder whether the architecture of tourism ought to be considered postcolonial. Perhaps, I tell myself, it is the expression of a weak and mild colonialism, one that is in any case founded on difference and distance with respect to the identity and mentality of the place. I ask myself this question every time I go to Sardinia. What is it for me, that image I have seen again and again over the course of my life, hundreds of times, arriving and leaving, that succession of gray mountain crests on the horizon of which I know neither the height, nor the substance, nor even how far away they are? What is my house to the guides who drive their boats noisily in front as they take tourists on trips around the archipelago? Just how great is the distance that still today separates me from this island? The architecture of tourism has never been assimilated by Sardinia, and the architecture of Sardinia has never really opened its doors to tourism.

Sardinia has a history, even if all too many have described it and continue to think of it as an empty island without one. There are few records of Sardinia's distant past, and in this respect there is not much of which we can be certain, but this is in no way true of the island's recent history. The last century has seen the arrival of industries, water reservoirs, ports, tourism, international transport, gastronomy, motorways, new landscapes ... The last century of Sardinian history has seen disappearances and appearances at the social, economic, and geographic level. It is following in the tracks of the writers Grazia Deledda, Gavino Ledda, and Salvatore Satta that this story must be told.

2 The Purchase

I was five years old, in 1964, when my parents bought a rocky piece of land from local shepherds. It was close to Palau, had no beach, and sat right underneath the Roccia dell'Orso. The land was then split into four lots, two of which ended up in my father's hands and two in those of a trusted partner and friend, Piero Paccagnella. The place was given the Homeric name of Porto Ulisse, a name that today, after the passage of over fifty years, is beginning to appear on some maps in an official guise. My family had already spent some time in the north of Sardinia; we had stayed for two summers (1963–1964) at the Hotel Moresco in Santa Teresa di Gallura, overlooking the beautiful beach of Rena Bianca, with the cliffs of Bonifacio, the coast of Corsican France, visible in the distance. My father spoke every so often of Capo Caccia to the west of Alghero and Capo Coda Cavallo to the south of Olbia, where he had probably gone to explore and sniff out what was really happening on the spot, not trusting in hearsay. The British, those notorious colonizers, had landed at Alghero in 1955, and this had received a lot of coverage in the media. In 1963—I think—my parents had bought a small plot of land at Liscia di Vacca near Porto Cervo, on which to build themselves a house by the sea. Some close friends of theirs (René and Gisele Podbielski) were directly involved in the founding and development of the Costa Smeralda, a grand real estate project spearheaded by Karim Aga Khan, specifically for the international jetset. But my parents' infatuation with the Costa Smeralda lasted only a few months. They sold the land they had just bought, making a profit, as soon as they realized that the site was one of the few on the coast exposed to the full force of the fierce west wind, and that the Costa Smeralda with its plans for golf courses, boutiques, and yachts was not what they were looking for inside and outside themselves. They were after something different, and perhaps unique.

According to family mythology it was at this point, still in 1963, that they began to look for something quite unlike Liscia di Vacca. They did this in the only way you can reconnoiter a coast, from the sea, and just as explorers in search of a safe haven had done for millennia. With the difference that my parents were not searching for a safe stretch of coastline, but its opposite, that is to say a stretch of coast that was dangerous and inaccessible, as they thought that only this would be able to guarantee them the isolation they were seeking for the future. So they went as far as Golfo Aranci in the vicinity of Olbia, and there they asked a sailor-fisherman who owned a sturdy wooden *gozzo*, as the typical fishing boats are called, to take them by sea to Santa Teresa, in the north, allowing them to scout around sixty kilometers of coastline. On the stalls lining the banks of the Seine in Paris, my father had bought the original French edition of the *Itinéraire de l'île de Sardaigne, pour faire suite au Voyage en cette contrée* written a century earlier by General Alberto della Marmora in 1860. It was this account that inspired the starting point for my parents' reconnaissance. Della Marmora says: "... the Golfo degli Aranci is the only large port on the whole of the eastern coast of Sardinia between Cagliari and the Strait of Bonifacio, and the only place where any vessel plying the Tyrrhenian Sea between Italy and Sardinia can find shelter if necessary."

Many of the stretches of the coastline that my parents saw on this trip were not served by road, but for the moment this was not a worry. They rounded the alluring Capo Figari with its amber-tinted cliffs and lighthouse and began to patiently make their way along the continual protuberances and indentations, headlands, and bays, that define the jagged shoreline of the Costa Smeralda. Snorting noisily and spitting out the dark and stinky fumes of a diesel engine, the *gozzo* explored this sheltered sea, that paradise on a human scale that was the Costa Smeralda, trying to see if there were still any points that would be hard to reach by the ambitious development projects under way. My parents said to themselves: "The whole coast is low-lying. In the future, it'll be easy to build on because it's easy to reach from both land and sea. It's certainly not made for captains courageous!" Almost all of the Costa Smeralda faces east and with its many beaches is well protected from strong currents or large rollers, as well as being sheltered in general from the dominant winds, the Maestrale from the northwest, and the Ponente from the west. They thought: "It's a coast with lots of qualities, a bit like the Caribbean, which is ideal for someone who already has in mind a major and multifaceted real estate scheme, with houses, villas, villages, hotels, harbors, marines, beaches, swimming pools, nightlife, and chic stores, for the young and the retired, and moreover close to an airport. But we did the right thing to sell up at Liscia di Vacca."

My parents saw things clearly, from their perspective. They went past Marinella, Porto Rotondo, Portisco. After the very early years of adventure, the Costa Smeralda today is a schizophrenic world, at once modern and picturesque, visionary and self-referential, elegant but vulgar, with an architectural style and a look of its own, somewhere between Zorro and Santorini. You could say that it is a world out of this world, a bubble in a bubble. At Cala di Volpe, they saw the building site of the hotel of the same name, viewed this time from the turquoise sea and not from the land. They realized that eventually it was going to turn into a whimsical château, a fanciful folly of organic and cavernous spaces; they smiled in awe and amusement. Its architect, Savin Couelle (1929–2020), born into the profession, already had a certain amount of experience in the world of movie sets and interior decoration when he designed it; in its eccentricity the Hotel Cala di Volpe is a visionary masterpiece that perhaps ought to be listed as worthy of preservation for its architectural merits.

Heading north at an average speed of six knots an hour, the *gozzo* (with her skipper keeping an eye out for shoals, perhaps after throwing out some trolling lines) slipped past places that in later years would become familiar to newspaper reporters and writers of society columns: Romazzino, the Golfo Pevero, Porto Cervo, Liscia di Vacca, Capo Ferro (with its fine lighthouse), Poltu Quatu, Baja Sardinia, Cala Bitta, Cannigione, Tanca Manna, Barca Bruciata, Le Saline, and finally Capo d'Orso (where there is another fine lighthouse). All names whose origin we wonder about today. The toponymy of this stretch of coast has not yet completely stabilized even now, and still fluctuates like the sea; the few names that have been present on the charts for some time (mostly drawn up by the British Navy) are today flanked by indigenous ones in the Sardinian tongue, names of an Anglophone taste, and others that have sprung out of nowhere in the heads of marketing experts. Observing the timeless and somewhat disquieting blank space of the coast, my parents came at last to realize just how geographically introverted Sardinia was and the extent to which the island's peoples had been ignoring their sea for millennia. For shepherds the coast was too rocky, and the pastures there were too poor; even though teeming with fish, the sea was not much use because the coast offered few havens. Arzachena did not even face onto the gulf of the same name. At Barca Bruciata they went to take a look at Casa Zanuso, the holiday home of the brother of the architect Marco Zanuso that was nearing completion: a courageous building halfway between a kind of primitive brutalism and the monumental classicism of Louis Kahn, a house that instead of a living room had a patio covered with a cane pergola. They admired its radical and spartan spirit, though it went too far for them. (The Hotel Cala di Volpe and Casa Zanuso were both published in 1964 by the Milanese architecture magazine *Casabella Continuità*, in the second of two monographic issues devoted to the coasts of Italy.)

That fateful day they rounded Capo d'Orso around the middle of the afternoon; the skipper turned the helm to alter course and head west. At that point they were rather wet, fed up, and demoralized, because the day was drawing to a close and they still hadn't found anything convincing, anything different from what they were already familiar with. They spoke to each other in English so as not to be understood. The sun was sinking and was going to set in fiery red right behind the port of Palau; only then did they realize that from the Costa Smeralda, which they had just left behind them, the setting sun could not be seen. "What a terrible thing! An absurdity!" declared my mother, who didn't mince her words and took everything to extremes. By way of compensation, they began to breathe the fresh breeze from the northwest, the sea grew choppy, a current made its presence felt, and the prow started to throw up some real spray. Now my parents were passing through a channel, almost a river given the strength of the current, as my brother Annibale (known as Bani), a skilled sailor, has always maintained; to port lay Sardinia proper, to starboard the island of Santo Stefano, still uninhabited at the time (now a large hotel-resort is open in the summer). In the distance, beyond another lighthouse, the one at Punta Sardegna, they caught a glimpse of the open sea in the Strait of Bonifacio.

Capo d'Orso, or "Bear Cape," is a large rocky lump, threatening to passing sailors who always like to keep a safe distance from it. Della Marmora again:

> The Capo dell'Orso gets its name from a granite rock that is located almost at its tip and that, observed from a certain point, to be precise from the side of La Maddalena, looks like a bear and even a polar bear. ... The rock already presented this extraordinary likeness some two thousand years ago, for Ptolemy, in his *Geography*, refers to the place as the 'promontory of the bear.'

In short the bear is a distinctly mental image, and can only be recognized as such from a particular position, at a certain distance, under the right light and if you're in the right mood, which means practically never. Nonetheless, for many years the bear has been a favorite subject of postcards. Sculptural rocks form this promontory that stands out strongly in the landscape, and which has neither beaches nor a sandy seabed at its feet. There were no roads

The Orso—postcard.
Archive Sebastiano Brandolini.

along the coast but there was a dirt road just a little way inland, my father realized, looking at the map he had brought with him in his bag, linking Palau to the hamlet of Capo d'Orso; this is a handful of modest rural houses that face inland, as if turning their back on the cold winter winds, occupying a col one hundred or so meters above the level of the sea. My father politely asked the sailor if he could go nearer to the shore and, with care, come almost close enough to touch the unbroken succession of large granite boulders that line this part of the coast. I doubt that my parents were able to set foot on land on that occasion, and I doubt whether anyone had ever done so before; what were to become, for all intents and purposes, our rocks would remain virgin for a few more days. From close up, however, the rocks appeared even more striking and sensual than from afar. My mother asked the skipper to turn off the noisy engine, as the sea was almost flat. Here and there lay tiny islets, looking like toys. The water is deep here and the desire to swim is only natural; the granite is solid, smooth, and flush with the water. There is even a natural swimming pool, something truly exceptional. Alongside, two phantasmagorical rocks seem to have come straight out of a geological manual of the absurd, so strange that we humans, hypnotized, find it hard to look at them. They are two works of natural engineering: one is a sphere and the other a tongue, and both are suspended above the water. My parents couldn't believe their eyes; to them this place looked like a true apparition. The place seemed a concentrate of all the stimuli and synesthetic impressions that landscape can convey: images, scents, noises, and tactile sensations. The die was cast, the decision taken, and the painstaking search for the right location had been rewarded. In short, a day well spent.

At Palau in those years you could build anywhere, and so my father, at that moment, did not envisage complications of a bureaucratic, planning, or administrative nature, and in fact there were none. Holiday homes were not perceived as a risk and still less as a potential threat to the environment. In those years, the only National Parks in Italy were those of the Gran Paradiso, Abruzzo, the Circeo, and the Stelvio; the local one of the Arcipelago di La Maddalena was not established until thirty years later, in 1994. The only constraint was the publicly owned coastal strip, about twenty meters wide, that could not be built on; but this was not a problem as the strip was filled with rocks anyway.

At this point the sun really was about to set, and not much time was left for them to reach Palau, a couple of nautical miles away, a journey of about twenty minutes including the entry into port. Palau was a small village consisting of a single, straight street, nothing more than the terminal of the ferry for the island of La Maddalena. For themselves and the sailor, my father had already booked two rooms at the Hotel Serra on Via Nazionale, a three-star establishment and the only one in the place during those years. For dinner, they would have gone to eat fish at Franco's, at the junction between Via Nazionale and Via Capo d'Orso. They canceled the second leg of their trip along the coast to Santa Teresa and the next day returned to the Podbielskis, friends they were staying with at Liscia di Vacca, happy with the results of their expedition. From there they called their trusted surveyor Azara to find out how best to go about buying the land. They also had to call their friend Piero Paccagnella, to see if he really wanted to be a partner in the adventure that was looming on the horizon. The evening before they had been able to discover that the whole of the stretch of coast they were interested in was the property of the many-branched Filigheddu family of Palau. They promised each other that in a few days they would go to Palau to find out more, and to see if anything interesting was going on in the area and who was really in charge of things.

Aerial view of the house.
© Waterfront Italy/John Bracco.

3 *My Parents*

My father Brandolino was the first-born of an aristocratic Venetian family, the Brandolini d'Adda. Even many years
after leaving Venice (he lived there until he went to study agricultural science in Bologna, not long after the end of the Second
World War), he was still a clearly recognizable figure when walking at a rapid pace though its *calli*, and was greeted by friends of
the same generation with respect and affection. His tall frame,
snow-white hair, and hooked nose were unequivocal marks of dis-
tinction. His father's sister, Vendramina Marcello del Majno, who
lived her whole life behind La Fenice and was a well-known per-
sonage before, during, and after the war for both her Fascist political sympathies and her generosity toward the Jewish community,
which she expressed without reservation. The story goes—and
it's probably true—that my father and mother met at Harry's Bar
in Venice and that it was there, with Ernest Hemingway already
tipsy on Bellini cocktails just a few tables away, that they fell in

love. I have in my possession a small double portrait—frontal and in profile in the Renaissance manner—that my mother made of Hemingway, autographed by the writer, who added "Very beautiful!" and underlined it. My mother Yasmin Petersen, tall and ebullient, was South African, of Boer origin although she spoke English as her mother tongue, and a talented painter. Immediately after the war she went off to explore—*comme il faut*—"la bella Italia," and setting out from her base in Florence went to see and study the works of art of the Renaissance, especially those of the early Renaissance. Among her favorite painters: Duccio, Giotto, Sassetta, Fra Angelico, Masaccio, Piero della Francesca, Giovanni Bellini, Botticelli, and Carpaccio. She was just as familiar with the painters who came after, but was less fond of them. Between the late forties and mid-fifties, like millions of other people, she suffered from tuberculosis of the lungs and was a patient for several years in the Abetina of the monumental Ospedale Morelli, a sort of modern castle at Sondalo in Valtellina, in the Rhaetian Alps just north of Milan and about a hundred kilometers south of Davos. At L'Abetina in 1953 she read Thomas Mann's *The Magic Mountain*, set in Davos, a book that for her became the parallel diary of her own firsthand experience and a push in the direction of a better world. This is how Mann explained the sense of *The Magic Mountain* in a lecture given at Princeton in 1939, and I like to think that it tells us something about the meaning that Sardinia had for my parents: "... for by depicting the hermetic enchantment of its young hero in timelessness, [the book] strives by its artistic means to annul time through the attempt to bestow full presence in every instant upon the musical and hypothetical world that it embraces and to create a magical 'nunc stans.'"

Brandolino and Yasmin got married in 1951 in South Africa, where they were thinking of putting down roots. At Hermanus, about fifty kilometers east of Cape Town, the Petersens had a house by the sea, surrounded by large rocks. Here, my parents escaped a difficult family situation that had developed at Cison di Valmarino, some seventy kilometers north of the Venetian lagoon, where my grandfather Annibale still lived in the family's medieval-Renaissance castle, sold to the Salesians a few years later. In the fifties the racial laws and apartheid started to come into effect in South Africa, and

30

so my parents, unable to bear the injustice, decided to go back to Italy. I don't know if at that point my father left behind the Fiat Topolino he had brought with him. But I do know that aboard the ship on the return voyage, as it was Carnival time when they passed through the stretch of the Red Sea off the coast of Egypt, a contest was held for the best costume, and my father won first prize thanks to my mother's idea of dressing him up as a mummy.

Back in Italy, my father realized that if he were to retreat to the countryside, to the family house at Cison, and live the life of a count, within a few years he would end up more or less penniless, a common fate in those years among many impoverished aristocratic families of the Veneto. Around the time my brother Annibale (1957) and I (1959) were born, my father moved to Milan, initially by himself and later joined by the rest of us. First we lived in a rather down-market apartment block on Via Melchiorre Gioia and shortly afterward in a fine building on the corner of Corso Venezia and Via Palestro, opposite the Giardini Pubblici and next to Villa Reale. The gardens contained a zoo, the Natural History Museum (nineteenth century, in a Romanesque style), and the Ulrico Hoepli Planetarium (twentieth century, designed by Piero Portaluppi). These three places left something of a mark on me.

My grandfather, after gambling away almost everything he possessed, took his own life at Brusson in Val d'Aosta in 1961; it was a dramatic event, but one that, at least in the way I imagine the order of events, opened the doors to Sardinia. If things in Veneto had gone the way they were supposed to, without a trauma of this gravity, Sardinia would probably never have presented itself as a dream, as a necessity, as redemption, as flight. From 1960 to 1988 my parents lived in Milan, where my father worked for Selezione dal Reader's Digest, the Italian offshoot of the great US publisher of popular material that went bankrupt when the digital revolution appeared on the horizon. In Milan my mother painted, diligently, methodically, and with few distractions; my father, in the little free time he had from work, wrote poems, often hermetic and filled with plays on words, that revealed his feelings and his playful side. Together they produced several books and carried out artistic projects. My father died in 2001, my mother in 2012.

They surrounded themselves with things of quality. It was in their genes and their personalities. From the panoramic position of the family castle (renamed today Castebrando) high up on a hill above Cison, and down below, in the house in the middle of the village (still called the Casagrande, the "Big House"), the family had always possessed fine furniture and beautiful objects, but sober and not ostentatious ones, of no particular value. Beautiful silver plates, arms in memory of the lineage's martial past, a few good paintings, some Empire furniture, even some handsome service pieces (like the ones made by the Shakers), along with splendid *maremmani* sheepdogs and long-haired cats. For them quality was more important than beauty. Things, whether costly or cheap, always had to be well made, which meant: sturdy, well finished, unpretentious, with a sense of respect for the passage of time. Even though they came from different social backgrounds, my father and mother saw eye to eye on the fact that superficiality, inaccuracy, and lack of attention were not merely shortcomings but true vices. Although they were well aware that the passing of time, with the changes it brings, was something inexorable (they had firsthand experience of this), it didn't bother them at all. Indeed they were farsighted enough to be able to distinguish changes for the better from those for the worse; they were not conservatives and still less snobs. Close-knit, they saw the Casagrande as something that needed constant renovation, and so they bought new things and gave away old ones, in order not to yield to stagnation. They didn't give a damn about nostalgia and laughed at the very idea. For them, life was a series of decisions that had to be taken. While this created a sense of indissoluble complicity between them and let them forge lasting friendships with a few lucky people, it put others in the shade and led to frequent moments of embarrassment with those who were perhaps fond of them but were kept at a distance. Even some of their untouchable friends could fall from grace over the slightest thing, only to find themselves once back in favor later on. They had no halfway friends, with both merits and defects. In my mother's vision of the world, you were either in or out, and there were no shades of gray.

Life itself had to be a project, made up in turn of plans: the plan of a place to live, of a journey, a concert, an exhibition, a book, a walk, an invitation to dinner, a gift, even the plan to listen to a Bach fugue on the radio. Sometimes there was a slightly military atmosphere at the Casagrande, as it was absolutely necessary to avoid the day being wasted, passing without "getting something done" as they used to say. For guests there were times and customs to be respected, otherwise their presence might have been an unwelcome disruption. Idleness was permitted, but it too had to be planned. Around eight o'clock on summer mornings everyone would gather for breakfast at the marble-topped table in the kitchen, and then go their separate ways to carry out their respective missions; shortly before midday we would converge on the pool to swim and sunbathe (anyone who failed to turn up would be called until they came); then, after an abundant and excellent lunch under the great horse chestnut tree in the garden (the vegetables, fruit, and chickens were all raised at home), the members of the family would retreat again into isolation. Moments of common and individual life alternated at a familiar rhythm, one that was also marked by the loud tolling of the bells on the nearby campanile of the parish church; a church where next to the altar sits our large family coat of arms, red and white and decorated with abundant stuccoes. My mother and father concentrated on their work—she on painting and he on writing—until shortly before dinnertime; they did this for themselves more than for others. During the winter and the in-between seasons, instead of the swimming pool we went for a walk in the woods above the village, which had once all been the property of the family, in the company of our *maremmani*, a handsome breed of dog but one whose behavior was at times unpredictable. There was something of the monastic and sacred about the life my parents led. They were the first to pay a high price for this schematic and rather idealistic vision. Fortunately their rituals and limitations did not get the better of the quality of their projects: places, books, works of art, objects, music, human relations, laughter, and many animals, including dogs, parrots, cats, rabbits, turtles, and doves.

The walled garden—which my father fittingly defined in a volume of verse as a *hortus conclusus*—and the Casagrande in Cison are worthy of a few more words. Together they do not form a homogeneous work of architecture, but a hybrid one, made up of different pieces mixed together and superimposed: Casagrande is at once house, villa, palazzo, farm, storehouse, workshop, holiday home, and place of residence. The various pieces—the rural parts, the original servants' quarters, the neoclassical wing from the nineteenth century, the porticos, the granaries—abut one another gracefully and are bound closely together by the outer wall of the garden, which contains them in a block isolated from the rest of Cison, *conclusus* in fact. The only entrance faces onto Cison's square, along with the church, the town hall, a small theater, and another building that used to belong to the Brandolini family but later passed to the Marcello del Majno and today is owned by the Colomban, the current proprietors of the castle. As has always been the case, some parts of the Casagrande are lived in, while others are used more for pleasure and entertainment, or as accommodation for the servants, or for work and self isolation, be it intellectual or manual. More than half of the buildings were once employed in farming, an activity that has ceased today but that up until the 1950s was the source of the family's feudal wealth. What is used today as a garden once served agricultural purposes, such as threshing grain or growing cereal; the gigantic granaries as big as tennis courts that form its backdrop were used in the past to store hay and corn, and vegetables were laid out on trellises for the winter. Then there were the cellar, carpentry shop, rooms for the silkworms, a storehouse for farming implements, stables, a workshop, and the dark cavern of a blacksmith; each had a distinctive smell of its own. There was a garden for vegetables and flowers which also housed hens, ducks, and geese, a few fruit trees, and a small greenhouse. The vegetable garden has always been a *hortus conclusus* within the *hortus conclusus* of the main garden. The walls, built of stone and then plastered, create a sense of beauty and isolation and give meaning to the property. In keeping with the Anglo-Saxon tradition, my mother arranged huge vases with complex arrangements of cut flowers, defying the laws of equilibrium and gravity. There are also some very big trees in the garden: a plane whose muscular branches loom dangerously over the roofs, a horse chestnut that in the summer offers providential shade and in the fall drifts of leaves and nuts, two odorous ginkgoes, and two scented limes. The garden belongs to the house in the same way a cloister belongs to its monastery, and is informal all year round. Tending it as much as needed, my parents made sure that the garden—which some erroneously call a "park," making the same mistake as those who call the house a "villa"—did not degenerate into something decorative or frivolous. We played soccer and badminton in it, and it was big enough to stroll in, giving us the pleasant sensation of being isolated but not imprisoned.

Brandolino and Yasmin had clear ideas about contemporary art, but not where it came to contemporary architecture, and as a consequence rarely passed judgment on it. They had good taste, but no specific understanding of it. In Milan, they thought the Pirelli Tower "elegant," unlike the other skyscrapers of the same years, which they dismissed as "shoeboxes." They liked the PAC (Padiglione d'Arte Contemporanea), in part because its architect Ignazio Gardella was a friend. For them, the Centre Pompidou was "fun" and the Pyramid of the Louvre "clean." Places were more important to them than buildings, and they drew real inspiration from them. Places did not appear in front of them by chance; they discovered them and created them in their own image, and then they looked after them continuously, as if they were sacred fires. For them, the personality of the place and the personality of the inhabitant went hand in hand. They liked the archaic, what came before the classical. Their sources of inspiration at the Casagrande were: the plane tree, the vegetable garden, the pairings of contemporary and antique art, the dogs, the cold rooms, the dark red shutters, and the lightning rod embellished with the coat of arms. What they liked about their pied-à-terre in Milan was the fact that they were on the top floor, the double exposure, the squeals of the trams, the foliage of the trees, the grocery on the doorstep, the built-in closets for storing the paintings, the fact that the photographer Gabriele Basilico had his studio on the ground floor. They took inspiration from ordinary, everyday things rather than from the extraordinary and unique, and this was a small luxury they allowed themselves. Over the thirty years or so in which they lived in Milan, from 1960 to 1990, they went to exhibitions and theaters to "feed" their minds; they had no need to chase after novelties or continual distractions in order to find out what they really liked. They relished reiterations, to such a degree that when something became a regular habit—the same walk, the same restaurant, the same shade of color, the same hour of the day—they would enjoy it more each time, as if life were enriched not by additions but by repetitions.

I am in Liguria at the beautiful house of an English friend, which I have renovated for her. It's a clear day and Corsica is on the horizon, although the doubt remains that it is just the mist, an illusion.

—"Why do you Anglo-Saxons love Italy so much?"

—"It's always been like that. For us, the Grand Tour never ended. What we love about Italy is the authenticity, the food, the climate, the friendliness. There are lots of beautiful gardens in England, but you certainly can't live in the open. To the British, Italy seems simple."

—"What you say appears to me to be an illusion, like the profile of Corsica. I don't know whether your Italy is the same Italy as the one we Italians know. But you're in excellent company, for Goethe, when he made his way comfortably by carriage down from the Brenner Pass, made exactly the same mistake!"

—"There is none of this in England. Here in Italy everything is a marvel. In the North of Europe you don't have this light and this air, it's almost all new and banal. Up there people drink wine to get drunk, not to be merry."

—"Would you be offended if I were to tell you that, in spite of everything, I think that in the end you are still something of a tourist?"

—"Yes, I am a little offended by what you say, if that's what you really believe. I think you're saying it to provoke me, as you often do. I was a tourist years ago, but I don't think I am anymore. I try to blend in with the locals, although I know it's not easy. With Brexit, we are even asked to stand in a separate line at the airport. And you, aren't you a bit English too?"

—"It's true … My mother was South African, kind of Anglo-Saxon; in this, she was a bit like you. History repeats itself in subtle ways. But for my mother the Mediterranean was above all a cultural aspiration, rather than a climatic one."

Arriving at Porto Ulisse by sea was fairly simple, as my parents had discovered. But getting there by land proved more complicated. From Palau it was an orienteering course, a minor test of character. The journey made by my parents a few days after their boat trip was by foot, through the yellow fields used for pasture, scrambling over a series of Sardinian dry-stone walls, and crossing two small valleys carved out by seasonal streams flowing from the rocky lump of the Orso. Toward the end of that summer in 1963, the cows and goats were gaunt, their sharp bones carved like those of the animals in Picasso's drawings of Andalusia. In the end, tired out, they succeeded in reaching the same point that they had identified from the *gozzo*. They were covered with scratches, especially on their ankles and forearms, but reassured. Thinking it over quickly, they persuaded themselves that from the main road it would be possible in some way to cut a new road for about a kilometer until it reached the land they wanted to buy, and that this land was not too steep. The walk had also made them realize that in this landscape it was difficult to judge both distances and dimensions with the naked eye, and that in a sense distances and dimensions are the same thing.

Today, anyone arriving by car for the first time has to follow my directions, because if you get lost it is hard to get your bearings again. The house's isolation means that getting there is an achievement and requires the passing of six tests, more like acts of faith than trials: 1) finding the right road out of Palau, which is not the one indicated on the signs; 2) continuing along the asphalt road even though it seems to be heading inland; 3) proceeding trustingly along the dirt road to Porto Ulisse, even if it's already dark; 4) getting out of the car, opening and closing the iron gate, even though there's no padlock; 5) after arriving at the end of the road, convincing yourself you've reached the right place; 6) walking calmly down the path paved with stone, for having doubts would mean you'd have to walk back up. Each of the stretches that make up the route (the asphalt road, the dirt road, the stone pathway) is a regression from civilization and a step toward a primordial, archaic state.

The road that leads from Palau to Capo d'Orso, asphalted sometime around 1970, runs east along a stretch of gentle coastline, passing by a cemetery, a campsite, a group of small villas with gardens, a boathouse, and a former military blockhouse that has now been turned into a mini-resort for retired navy officers. The road still has tight bends, although vague attempts have been made to straighten them out over the years; it has a steep uphill stretch, a pedestrian crossing with poor visibility, and an intersection. Accidents are frequent in the summer because the traffic, inattentive and careless, is made up of people walking or running, bicycles, motorbikes, public transport, campervans, and of course cars. The Orso, present in all the tourist guidebooks, is a landmark and attracts families, even if it is in the wrong position on satnavs. Fifty years ago, when the Mediterranean scrub was low and sparse, the views of the archipelago from the road were panoramic. Today this is no longer the case. The road was built for vehicles to meet military and naval needs, serving the houses of Capo d'Orso and the fort and lighthouse of the same name, as well as the activity of the *saline* (saltworks) below. Today the road ends at Capo d'Orso, fizzling out into a multitude of dead ends.

Exactly three kilometers along the asphalt road from Palau, my directions tell you to turn left, and it is here that the dirt road begins; the junction is an integral part of the house's landscape project, according to my son Martino. The dirt road transmits vibrations and wakes our senses, requiring a respectful handling of the car's wheel, brakes, tires, clutch, and gears; the horn needs to be used but with discretion; anyone on a motorbike has to be even more careful. The Mediterranean scrubland, perennially in search of sunlight, invades the roadway and threatens to scratch the bodywork. Driving down this stretch of road is a pleasure, with its ups and downs and constant bends that resemble a roller coaster: gentle descent, steep descent, flat along the valley bottom, steep climb, flat on a ridge, steep descent with gate, steep climb, gentle climb, flat on the space for parking. Sharp bend to the left, straight stretch, curve to the right, curve to the left, sharp bend to the right, sharp bend to the left, gentle curve to the left, bend to the right, straight stretch, curve to the right, curve to the left, curve to the right, curve to the left, straight stretch, curve to the left, area with a small roundabout. At certain points its bed is made of fine sand, at others of coarse gravel, and every so often a stone protrudes from the ground; if it rains runnels of water form, flowing through mini-canyons, sometimes quite deep. A few years ago two cars whose drivers were having fun raising trails of dust behind them collided head on, without anyone getting hurt given the low speed; no more than fifty meters of road are ever visible at a time. It feels like you're in the mountains, the altitude and the distance from the sea are not apparent. The Orso—unrecognizable from here—rises on our right while on our left we can glimpse the blue of the sea. The actual size of the rocks is deceptive, and some of the small ones look big. The nature here is wild, not artificial and tamed like the backdrop you see in the advertising for Sardinian resorts.

The dirt road ends at the car park, a sunlit piece of flat ground probably created by tamping the rubble from the building site, although this is something I can't be sure of. Once, in the days before air conditioning, a shed made of posts, beams, and a cane roof stood here, first for one and then for two cars, to stop them getting boiling hot in the sun. The Sardinian climate wore down the shed, and then the Maestrale, the fierce northwest wind, swept it away. No one bothered to rebuild it. By way of compensation, a holm oak that had with difficulty found shelter next to one of the posts has been facilitated in its growth and has become what is today a small tree at the geometric center of the area, which has in turn become a mini-roundabout. I have some affection for this roundabout, as it occupies a strategic position on our approach to the house; it is set right between the colossal rock that looms above it and the sea below, and puts them in contact. The rock hangs over it in alarming fashion, with numerous crows flying around and making a racket; on nights when the moon is full it reflects the light and renders the headlamps of the car unnecessary. Caves at the foot of the roundabout run back up the mountain. Some of the mountain's walls appear slimy and damp as if they were gigantic limestone stalactites, while others seem to have been worked with a bush hammer, as if made up of cubes and rhombuses separated by horizontal and vertical fissures to form a lattice, a sort of *cretto*, as Alberto Burri called his memorable work of land art at Gibellina in Sicily. From a distance the rock appears firm, but if you look more closely you will see that it is crumbling and flaking, and that its erosion is producing sand which, with the help of the roots and leaves of the few plants that are able to grow here, will turn in a few centuries into soil. In his *Geography*, Ptolemy already wondered how long it would take for granite to change its appearance. This monochromatic wall is a monolith that is breaking up and splintering, and each piece of it reflects a different stage in its erosion.

A contrast to these dreamlike and supernatural dimensions, unmovable and insensitive to the variability of time and the seasons, is provided by the liquid expanse of the sea that spreads out below us like an unstable and volatile, impressionistic and changeable panorama. The water seeps between the islands of the archipelago, with Santo Stefano and La Maddalena in front, Caprera to the right, and Spargi to the left. It looks as if the water has been spilt; its tones shift with the movement of the sun and the clouds in the sky; from this distance the ripples of the waves are barely visible, but the sinuous lines of the currents stand out. The scorching hot sand of the parking area also contrasts with the water, cool by definition; it is a difference that pertains to the original idea of the house, for nothing in architecture is improvised or happens incidentally. Many things here, rather than having been designed in the traditional sense of the term, were conceived with foresight at the moment the land was purchased. From here we take the path that goes down to the house; we can't go wrong.

There are about fifty granite steps on this path, all made of split stone of different sizes, so that none of them are the same. It is not particularly steep, and the slope varies. Length of the path: one hundred meters. Drop: twenty meters. Three minutes to climb it, two to descend. The dense vegetation of the maquis, left to its own devices, is constantly changing. A juniper bush twenty centimeters from the path is something quite different from a holm oak shrub at fifty. The leaves and dry branches are only rarely swept up and removed. In winter, in the season of rains and mushrooms, the path turns into a torrent and occasionally the water even seeps under the door and makes its way into the house. In the spring the endemic orchids of Sardinia sprout between the stones. On the right-hand side, slanting walls of granite are inhabited by thousands of yellow, green, and gray lichens, proof of the cleanliness of the air. Better to talk little and concentrate: on the way down because you might slip or stumble; on the way up because you're short of breath. Barefoot, you are guaranteed distinctive tactile sensations and gratifications; the stones don't hurt. The path offers no views of the distant surroundings but only of what is close by, the undergrowth, which often goes unnoticed. The contrast with the parking area is evident; from one moment to the next we have passed from a panorama to a miniature, from a wide-angle to a telephoto lens, from sunshine to shade, from wheels to feet. The sudden contrasts are stimulating. The house is accessible only from here, by this path. We are obliged to leave the car up there, where it can no longer be seen, and we've already forgotten all about it. House and car are things that need to be kept separate, incongruous with one another. Not everyone enjoys having to carry shopping bags, heavy carts of water and wine, bags and suitcases down these steps, but it's a small price to pay if we really want isolation. At the end of the path appears a right angle of two walls, the corner of the house, with a bench next to it, should anyone wish to sit down. You enter through the door at the back, which is the main one; otherwise you continue down the path and

La Maddalena Archipelago—postcard.
Archive Sebastiano Brandolini.

alongside a wall in the direction of the sea ruffled by the wind, which we can see with the eyes, hear with the ears, and smell with the nose.

Doubtfully, two boys make their way down the path, with the whole colorful caboodle needed to spend a happy day by the sea. They are followed a few meters behind by two girls, who are trying not to be seen.

—"Hello, what the hell do you think you're doing here?"

—"Is it private property?"

—"Of course it's private property. Just like it says on the gate."

—"We didn't see that, and the gate was open anyway."

—"That's strange, I closed it ten minutes ago. I'm politely asking you to leave. It's private property here, no trespassing."

—"But since we've got this far, and it's hot today, can we at least go down to the sea and have a swim? We won't be a disturbance."

—"No, it's not allowed."

—"And if we go anyway, what are you going to do about it?"

—"Well, it would be rather unpleasant. I'd have to call the police."

—"So we are going to have to climb all the way back up this path? It was already hard work on the way down."

—"From the sea you can come whenever you want, because the coast is public property, but from the land no. Please come back when the house is empty. I give you my permission."

—"You won't even let us take a dip? Just an hour, and then we'll go."

—"No, not even a dip. Try to understand, we're here on vacation."

—"Ok, we'll leave."

—"Wait, let me at least give you a drink of water, because you're nice people and you must be dehydrated."

—"We needed that. The water is cool, very good. Thank you."

It is wind that shapes places, more than temperature. It is rare here for there to be no wind and even when it's not blowing it is present anyway, in the shape of a sleeping spirit. Describing it is almost impossible because you end up describing nothing more than its effects. In ancient times, it was never completely personified, and remained a spiritus, for it does not have a recognizable form. The locals never talk about it, for they are so accustomed to the wind that it wears them out. Everything here is steeped in it: the shape of the plants, the colors, the noise, the motions of boats, the workings of our head and our belly, our hunger and thirst, the times we choose for reading and repose. It could even be said that the form of the rocks is a self-portrait of the wind, with no sharp edges and modeled by endless curves, infinite shapes and shadows. The prevailing wind is the one from the west called Ponente (known in antiquity as Zephyrus), which leaves its mark on the day, on your well-being, and on the temperature. As soon as you wake up, and even before getting out of bed, the sounds and the humidity tell you the wind is blowing and what things are going to be like over the course of the day. In the evening, eating dinner with strong gusts of Maestrale from the northwest or with the sea as smooth as oil are two completely different experiences; in the first case the candles keep blowing out, in the second they stay lit. The wind alters odors, feelings, the weight of the body, and everything around us. It is the song of the Sirens, and can even drive us mad, as happened to Ulysses, who had himself bound tightly to the mast of his boat because he wanted to hear them sing. In contrast Timon, a Skeptic philosopher of ancient Greece, considered those who passed their life without disturbance to be happy, in a state of calm and absolute peace: "Sea flat on every side, without a breath of wind." Even more than a point of observation of the landscape, the house is an excellent wind gauge. As soon as you move away from the coast or downwind, by miracle it almost vanishes and everything changes: the temperature is different, you hear new noises and smell new scents, and no longer feel overwhelmed by the incontrollable forces of nature. To defend themselves from the wind and the currents, nearby ports like Palau, La Maddalena, and Porto Rafael are all located in sheltered positions.

When it blows, the Ponente enters with force from the west (that is, from the left), from the Strait of Bonifacio, wedging itself into the arm of sea about a kilometer wide that separates the islands of La Maddalena and Spargi from the peninsula of Punta Sardegna. In front of the house the sea, our sea, the *mare nostrum*, takes on a bright cobalt-blue hue and turns into a river, with a current against which it is almost impossible to swim or navigate. The waves, although not as big as in the open sea, are neurotic and noisy whitecaps and come in rapid flurries, one every five meters, one every seven seconds. Simply standing upright on the rocks is a precarious balancing act, and you must be ready for sudden gusts. Only the portico of the house offers the right degree of protection. When the wind is at its strongest boats disappear from the sea, and even the regular ferry service between La Maddalena and Palau is temporarily suspended. The laundry hanging on the line is beaten like a drum, drying in a few minutes if it doesn't first fly away. Don't even think about flying a kite. The place to go and sunbathe is downwind to the east, on an artificial solarium built of stone, but here too the gusts creep between the rocks and create unpredictable vortices. Where there are holes in the granite, the wind moans and howls. There is a resemblance between the forms of the granite on the foreshore and the shape of certain waves, so that they seem to have been modeled by the same choreographer; the Ponente is music. It drives the waves up against certain rocks with mathematical precision and regularity, and on their sides the waves draw sinuous and sensual forms, without leaving a trace. On the diving boards the spray makes luminous ghosts, rainbows in miniature. The more powerful waves beat out the rhythm of the passage of time, and the same movement is repeated hundreds of thousands of times a year. Diving and swimming among the billows is an electrifying thrill. The sky when the Ponente blows is clear, the air dry and cool. It takes about three days for a *ponentata*—usually due to a depression over the Sea of Sardinia (which also generates the Mistral in the Gulf of Lion)—to blow itself out; in short, when the Ponente rises you know more or less when it is going to die down. But it is not always so fierce, for it has many gradations and degrees; it can also be a breeze that lasts for just a day and disappears during the night.

The calm, the "sea like oil" of which Timon speaks, is the opposite of the Ponente, a respite from it. There would not be one without the other. This is due not so much to the absence of wind as to its temporary invisibility. Then the sea turns flat, devoid of any wave or motion, smooth as glass and completely transparent. It becomes a swimming pool at the moment just before people dive in. The water loses its materiality, defying our ordinary understanding of things. In this natural pool the cormorants pursue the fish at high speed; to catch them they go in ever tighter circles, and then suddenly turn right round and the fish swim straight into their mouths. On the rocky seabed the urchins, anemones, and sea cucumbers look as if they are on display in a showcase. On the surface of the water the wakes produced by sailboats, forced to rely on their engines, last for eternity before vanishing. The few fishermen watch from the shore in silence, trying to make out the passage of a school of mackerel or sardines, or the fin of a dolphin. Could the calm be unnatural weather, an ill omen, a trap? It never lasts long, just a few hours or at most half a day; it will disappear as soon as the land warms up and an offshore breeze rises.

Then there is the Levante, blowing from the east and which is often confused with the Scirocco that blows instead from the southeast, from Syria. Less frequent than the Ponente, it also lasts for about three days. These are hot, humid, and unpleasant winds; nothing dries, you sleep badly, feel listless and sweaty; you eat salad and drink water. Clouds bring the occasional downpour laden with sand. The color of the sea shifts between sky blue and gray, losing its glassy transparency and becoming mottled and almost lacustrine. The waves seem to arrive from many different directions at once, quarreling with one another and leaping up and down, as if startled. For some reason connected to the currents, various pieces of garbage that would normally stay out at sea arrive inshore. The air grows as hot as the African continent from which it comes and as saturated with moisture as the Mediterranean over which it passes. The water of the sea seems to heat up and grow heavy, turning into brine; swimming in it produces a different sensation, and you are more likely to encounter jellyfish.

Here you grow hypersensitive to the meteorological aspect of the landscape, as did many painters of the nineteenth century who became so obsessed with the weather that they turned it into a subject for their pictures: Constable, Turner, Sisley, Pissarro, and Monet, as well as the Italian Macchiaioli and the Scandinavian Impressionists. The weather of the moment, with its currents, winds, abrupt changes in humidity and temperature, and with its repercussions on the light and the colors, powerfully conditions our summer idleness and makes us lazily active. It seduces us, possesses us, and manipulates us. We no longer look for the weather forecasts that we follow on our smartphones in the city because the reality of what unfolds before us is better and more eloquent. Science is one thing, our perception of things another.

The house, built solely for holidays, is exposed to the weather, and that is how it was conceived by my parents, who were not architects. It occupies a precise place, has a precise form and a precise function, and none of these three can be modified. The small changes it has undergone in the fifty-five years of its existence concern secondary details, like the closets, the kitchen, a few windows, the retiling of the bathrooms, the elimination of the chimney on the roof. In essence it is exactly the same as it was in 1965, the first summer of its use. It has been spared substantial changes because my parents did not think of it as flexible or adaptable. Martino, my son, who is not an architect either, argues that it is an idea. As such it rejects the possibility of being altered, for better or worse. Anyone who decides one day to alter it will have to demolish it and start again from scratch, and then it will be another story and another idea.

The plan of the house is geometric, composed of two rectangles of equal base, one slightly higher than the other, unified to form a square. The two rectangles are located on different levels and since they are staggered do not overlap; they are set on a plot of land facing north, with a slope of about thirty degrees. The lower and slightly larger rectangle contains the living area; the upper and smaller rectangle houses the bedrooms. The landside wall of the living area coincides with the sea-side wall of the sleeping area. An internal staircase links the two levels, following the slope of the ground for the first part and then forking to form a T in order to reach the three bedrooms. On the lower story there is a portico with three arches. Just behind this is the living room-kitchen, and a study, bathroom, and storeroom located on the west side of the house. The upper floor contains the bedrooms, two on the east side and one on the west, connected by a corridor with a bathroom at either end. Each bedroom has its own window and two beds. Halfway up the stairs between the lower and upper level, a mezzanine acts as a junction for the different routes one takes inside the house; it faces onto the living room and contains a couch and writing desk. The staircase is scenic. Portico, living room-kitchen, staircase, and mezzanine form a single space.

A single pitch of the roof, parallel to the ground, connects the two levels spatially. Viewed from the sea, the house is composed of nothing but a portico, a roof, and two small towers. The perimeter of the square is practically devoid of doors and windows, and this gives it a grave and austere air, the look of a fort. *Monacale*, "monastic," my mother would have said, scrupulous in her choice of words even in Italian, despite English being her native language. At the rear, on the side facing the mountain, are the main door and a few honeycomb brise-soleil for ventilation. On the west side are more brise-soleil for the two bathrooms, and the door and window of the ground floor study. On the east side there is the fixed window of the living room-kitchen. The only external openings facing the sea are the three arches of the portico because those of the living room-kitchen (two French windows and a window) are set in an internal wall. The three windows of the three bedrooms give onto the roof, and so are not located on the perimeter.

The organization is plain and straightforward. I've often wondered how it was conceived and designed, and by whom. The fact that I don't know intrigues me, it is as if something important has eluded me. There is no sign of any effort having gone into its planning even though, observing the precision of the measurements and the harmony of the proportions, it seems unlikely that everything went smoothly over the course of its construction and there were no complications. How much ground was excavated to get things on the right level? How did they manage to get the height of the window sills in the bedrooms to coincide so precisely with the level of the roof beneath? How did they make sure that the mezzanine would function well as a spatial junction between the different levels? Were there working drawings, or just plans on a 1:100 scale and the rest improvised in situ, as was customary at the time? Did they excavate only in the area of the living room and the entrance at the rear, or for other parts of the house as well? Was an accurate survey carried out? Was a small study model made? Were alternatives or variations considered? The house could have been very different, both in plan and in elevation. Did someone check how much higher the volume would be than the profile of the landscape? Before breaking the ground were there beautiful rocks, luxuriant junipers, and turtle burrows on the site? I have no answers to these questions, not even hypotheses. In the family album, yellowing photographs show a miniature rack-and-pinion track that was laid during construction. Perhaps my mother, an artist with a good imagination, sketched the internal spaces and external views, in rapid and precise drawings of the kind she used to make. If she did, she would have thrown them away as soon as the house was finished. She never kept what she no longer needed; she always had everything under control.

It is a bare house, but not one without details. In all likelihood, the white window frames are a simplified version—mitered corners, no drips, single panes of glass without glazing beads—of what the local carpenter knew how to do. The Tizianella brushed steel handles, designed by Sergio Asti in 1961, came from Milan. I think that the external shutters, which are also white, must have been sketched by my mother because there is something Giottesque and archaic about their design, with their horizontal planks

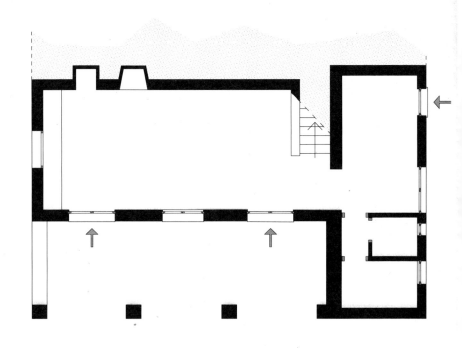

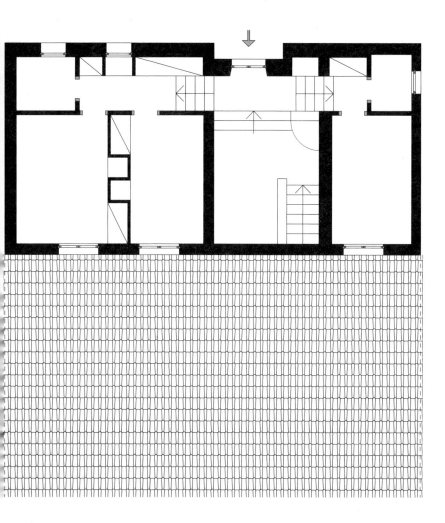

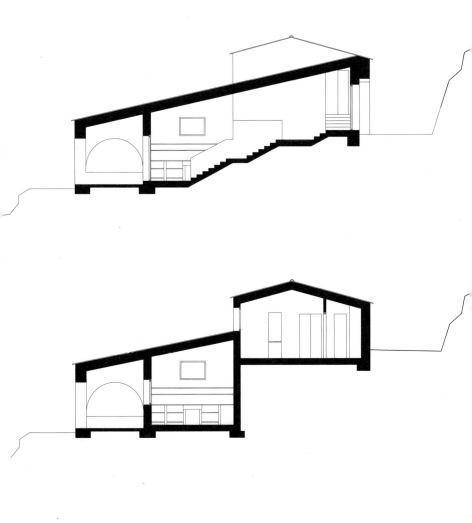

Cross-sections.
Archive Sebastiano Brandolini.

and stiffening diagonals. Apart from what could only be made of wood, everything is solid masonry. The shelves, full of books for summer reading and guides (on seashells, crustaceans, fish, plants of the Mediterranean maquis, the Nuragic culture, etc.), are built of masonry. The floors (except in the bathrooms) are covered with pale terracotta tiles, easy to wash with water; age has improved them, giving them a variegated patina. Guests ask me the name of the manufacturer and I tell them I have no idea, only that they don't come from Cerasarda, the ceramic company of the Costa Smeralda established by the Aga Khan. The color of the exterior—a pink that varies slightly every time it gets repainted—echoes the shades of the floor and the roof, and this makes the prismatic geometry of its volumes evident. Built out of a single material and all the same color, the house lacks a theory, but is a practical solution. The fact that it has no gutters or downspouts like many of the buildings of the Mediterranean is important. The thick walls convey a sense of solidity, of protection, and the very idea of shade and shelter from the wind. Although it faces north, it is as full of light as an artist's studio, and in a way that is exactly what it is. The direct light of the sun enters only obliquely and in summer, early in the morning and late in the evening.

The position of the geometric square plan has been determined with a precision that would not have been easy to achieve, even with a topographic survey accurate to the centimeter. That position is absolute and free of imperfections; its perimeter is like the frame of a picture, whose dimensions also determine its form and content. The house itself is set in the landscape like an electrical appliance in a kitchen; between those plants and those masses it cannot slip, deform its shape, move, adapt, or grow in any direction. It is the opposite of an organic house. The pathway running around its square is roughly paved with stones, protecting it from the risk of wildfire and underlining its austere and uncompromising relationship with the surroundings. Laid without any precise design, the pathway takes different forms on each side. At the front it is the *dehors* of the portico; on one side it is a gently sloping flight of steps, a continuation of the path descending from the parking area; on the other side there is a service area with a steep staircase, a cave, the garbage cans, and the clothes lines; and behind it is the main entrance surrounded by trees and shrubs. None of the four sides is free, because everywhere there are obstacles and boundaries: plants at the back, public land in front, rocks at the sides.

Lying down to read or doze on the mezzanine couch is a much cherished activity. From here you can command and control everything that happens, and from here nothing goes unnoticed. Anyone who manages to grab this privileged post can see (without being seen) whether the bedrooms are occupied, hear if someone is busy in the kitchen downstairs or walking in the portico, and tell if someone is using one of the three bathrooms. Look in one direction and you can just glimpse the sea; look the other way and you can perceive, through the main door, that the depth of the house can be measured in a single glance. The mezzanine is a boudoir on the edge of a precipice, and contrasts a sense of security with a sense of danger, as does the house as a whole.

Anyone withdrawing into one of the bedrooms, on the contrary, is completely isolated and not aware of anything that goes on elsewhere. The bedrooms are slightly different sizes, austere, and minimal, with a vague air of a hospital. I realized this once when, suffering from backache, I spent a few days in a horizontal position while a Syrian doctor from Palau came twice a day to give me an injection. The rooms are so empty that you get the impression a move is underway, even though there is no sign of disorder or the displacement of objects. Each one has four white walls, a window, and a shed-like ceiling; the only furnishings are beds, bedside tables, a wardrobe, a flat top, and a couple of chairs; everything strictly necessary to sleep well is there, and it's more than sufficient. In the summer, when the Scirocco brings muggy weather, a fan is enough. You don't need air conditioning. At night, anyone who can't sleep can climb through the window and onto the roof, sit on the roof tiles and gaze at the stars, trying to guess the time before going back to bed. Early in the morning, a blade of yellow light enters through the centimeter-wide fissures between the shutters and the edge of the wall. If you take a nap in the afternoon, you can't tell what time it is when you wake up. The fact that the windows have larger and more eccentric proportions than the norm and are set higher up than usual from the floor is enough to create a sense of disorientation and a feeling of uniqueness. The absence of balconies in front of the bedroom windows is deliberate and well thought-out. The *genius loci* entails mild privations. If there were balconies, the role of the portico as a common space for everyone and everything would be devalued and it would no longer be used. If there were balconies, the house would look like the ones designed by the *geometri* (building surveyors) and the roof would lose its sharp, clean appearance.

For my parents it made sense for all the windows to give onto the sea. They lived in gray Milan and dreamed about this view in the winter. On the lower floor the three openings of the living room face onto the sea, making it a panorama, while on the upper floor each window frames it, turning it into a picture. Almost always, as soon as you get up in the morning the windows are thrown open, and you fill your lungs. My mother and father regarded the landscape as their private garden. For them this was also a way of burying for good the problems of health and family they had had to tackle and overcome together at Cison di Valmarino and in Milan at the beginning of the sixties. The panorama represented a newly found freedom. Their new place was the beginning of a new adventure. With pride and mischief, they liked to compare their panorama with those of other houses built in the area in the same years: one was too far from the sea, another had little land and was in the lee of the wind, yet another had a small beach but its rocks were insignificant, one stood on a site that was too flat, from another you could see neither the sunrise not the sunset.

For us today things are different. We assign more importance to the location than the panorama. Sometimes we don't even open the windows, and perhaps at the end of the day realize we haven't even gone down to the sea but have remained in a state of perpetual semi-darkness, doing no more than reading a book. About ten years ago, to suit our lifestyle, we installed two new anti-panoramic windows, one facing east and the other west. The eastern one frames the sky and lets in the cold white light of the morning, while the western one looks straight onto a sloping surface of granite that reflects the warm and reddish light of the evening. The two windows relate to conceptual, immaterial, abstract situations. In short, with the passing of the years, the beauty of Porto Ulisse has changed. It is no longer the same as it was fifty years ago. I find myself ignoring the panorama that is all too familiar and that sometimes obsesses me; instead I am hypnotized by details, like the dance of the shadows, the effects of the light, the differences between early and late morning, the incomprehensible behavior of plants, the disappearance of certain insects, and the arrival of others never seen before. If the house is really an idea, then it is an idea whose strength has allowed it to adapt to different generations and multiple ways of life.

As for the furniture and other objects, over the years much has broken, been stolen, or simply disappeared, magically vanishing into thin air. The guiding thread in the choice of furniture has always been that it should be wooden and painted white, with the sole exceptions of the big table under the portico and the desk on the mezzanine, both made of untreated wood. Many of the pieces came from the Casagrande at Cison di Valmarino, and are functional items made of pine or fir: a dresser with two doors and a marble top from the kitchen, a rectangular chest for oats originally in the stable, some bedside tables with two capacious drawers lined with Varese marbleized paper, a few wicker garden chairs and a set of small, useful, and versatile rectangular or hexagonal tables. The desk on the mezzanine also comes from Cison; the drawers beneath the top and at the sides are mostly empty, containing at the most an old telephone directory, a list of emergency numbers, and a bunch of postcards that never got sent; the handles are made of brass and the top covered with baize. Then there are the pieces made by Sardinian carpenters, which have a linear design and are so heavy they're almost impossible to move. All of them are painted white too: a round dining table, a low round table for the living room, a rectangular table, benches of various lengths. The big table in the portico was made in Sardinia, and as it's always been there seems eternal. By some strange coincidence, the austerity of my family from Veneto ended up fitting in and blending with Sardinian sobriety, to the point of creating a new utilitarian and functional style. Even the *stazzi* of the Gallura region (vernacular and basic single-story countryside structures, much revered by Alberto Ponis) and the farmhouses of the Brandolini family in Veneto have some traits in common.

There have never been any special objects, but plenty of fine and durable ones. Lagostina pots and pans, Cerasarda decorative plates, Sambonet steel flatware, green drinking glasses from Empoli. At a certain point my mother splashed out and bought Artemide light fixtures in Milan; their plastic parts turned yellow but survived for a while, but the metal ones (even when made of stainless steel) rusted rapidly and did not last at all; as always it was the Sardinian climate that won. In the living room there were three collections of objects, none of them directly connected with Sardinia. Above the fireplace there was a parade of *cuchi*, ceramic whistles from Bassano del Grappa, originally intended for use as talismans, love tokens, children's toys or symbols of the breath of life; eventually they all broke. On the wall of the staircase there were about thirty metal fishing spears, all of different sizes and shapes in relation to their origin, the seabed and the fish to be caught, which my father had brought from various places around the world (there was even an Inuit one made of bone); one winter they were stolen and have never been replaced. On a masonry shelf that has now been demolished, there was a collection of seashells from the Atlantic and Indian oceans given to me and my brother by our maternal grandmother, souvenirs from faraway South Africa. Once we played a trick on the young son of some friends by leaving one of these exotic shells on the seabed close to the house for him to find. We saw his excited splashes in the water and then an arm emerged from the waves clutching the enormous shell. He even returned home to Milan with it, full of pride, and showed it to his classmates. The ruse was finally exposed by his teacher who declared it a remnant of the Tropics not the Mediterranean. When he discovered the truth the boy was very disappointed. The three collections reflected moments in the life of my family (Veneto, South Africa, travel), and enriched our new ties with Sardinia (the wind, fishing, the sea), making this a family home.

In random order, here is a list of other objects in the house. Two pictures of the *Madonna and Child* painted on glass, examples of Sicilian folk art. Engravings, collages, and drawings done by my mother (she was annoyed that these, despite the many burglaries, were never stolen). British chart of the Maddalena Archipelago. Physical map of Sardinia. Carapace of a sea turtle that we found dead in the sea (we never managed to get rid of the bad smell). Cotton carpet with floral motifs in light colors, hung for years above the fireplace, of unknown origin. Watercolor of a village in Provence, the work of Maurice van Essche (1906–1977), a Belgian artist who taught my mother painting at the Michaelis School of Fine Arts in Cape Town and a friend of Henri Matisse's who closely resembled Le Corbusier. Sardinian containers, baskets woven from rush and asphodel of various sizes (impossible to find today). Piece of gray driftwood, so smooth it resembles marble. Oval white stone (also looks like marble), weighing about a kilo, from a nearby beach. Recent cuttlebones. Spatialist *Amiantite* by Roberto Crippa. *Impronta* by Giancarlo Sangregorio, an artist who made sculptures out of a combination of wood and stone. Modular cabinet made of ivory-colored plastic, designed by Anna Castelli and manufactured by Kartell. An oil painting by my father, made in his youth, dated 1949 and depicting the Giudecca Canal in Venice, where he had lived during the war. A large black-and-white photograph by Davide Virdis of the arm of the sea between Capo d'Orso and Caprera. Juniper branch, pruned because it grew too close to the outside walls of the house. Pictorialist photograph by Domenico Riccardo Peretti Griva. Two engravings by the illustrator Alberto Longoni of Pinocchio at sea, underwater among little fish and on the surface just before he is swallowed by the Terrible Dogfish. They are all things whose subjects and materials are in tune with life in this place.

Reduced to its minimum terms, the house responds to three fundamental architectural questions: location, organization, and furniture. Once the site had been chosen, once it had been decided that the common spaces would be on the ground floor and the private rooms on the one above, and once a philosophy of interior decoration based on the exclusive use of white objects had been defined, the design of the house was complete for my parents, the leap of faith taken. Anyone who came afterward would have to ask the same questions and would have to give the same answers. Which friends to invite and which to exclude? What to expect from the holidays? What importance to assign to comfort and luxury? Is seasonality a weakness or a virtue? The domestic commandments have not changed with the years: do only what is strictly necessary, put aside any aspiration to alter things, cut down on consumption, let slowness prevail over efficiency, accept that the wind and the sun are going to decide when it is time to throw things away.

Two aesthetes, one an expert on works of art and the other on high fashion, have come to see us. They have traveled to the planet's special locations, know everyone and say what they think without compunction. For them beauty is life, but they are also tired of the ephemeral. They talk in animated fashion, interrupting each other.

—"What a place! It looks like a garden, with these rocks in miniature! It looks like a painting, with these arches! A Japanese haiku! Where does the sun set?"

—"The house is a device, a pretext. But for what?"

—"I don't know. Anyway it's bare, made to produce shade. Perhaps to eat in too, and sleep well afterward."

—"With friends, it would be an exquisite hangout for fun and pleasure, distilled in their essence. Don't you think?"

—"No, for me it would be a place in which to read long and mostly illegible books. *Ulysses* and the *Recherche* for me; the *Comédie humaine* and *The Hobbit* for you!"

—"It gives me goosebumps. We are surrounded by a forest, the plants come damn close. It instills a bit of fear, but the kind that reinvigorates. I'm reminded of the dark fairy tales of the Brothers Grimm."

—"Don't worry, there are two of us here. And for now only on a visit. When we come for a whole month, it'll be better if they are lots of us, but they should be the right people. Incredible, there seems to be no oven in the kitchen ..."

The house is an ideal place to bury yourself in a book, to the point where on some days it turns into a silent reading room, without anyone ever having planned it to be that way. In the summer a sort of dreamy laziness holds sway. There are different places where you can go to read, depending in part on what you're reading; there is a subtle pleasure in finding a possible match between location and book. You can choose the book first and then the place, or reverse the order, as you like. The portico already offers a fair number of possibilities. Seated at the table you can read facing the sea or with your back to it, and these two orientations say much about your mood. Then if someone, still in the shade of the portico, decides to read while sitting in an armchair, it means that the book requires less concentration. My preferred site for reading is in the portico, on the ledge of the lateral arch support. I lie down on the hard surface with my spine stretched straight and a cushion stolen from a chair folded in two behind my head. It's a position halfway between inside and outside, and just the right length and width for me. Only I like this place, and it's never already occupied. The almost twenty-meter-long granite bench just in front of the portico is another possibility if you want to lie down and read, but it's narrow and its surface of split stone can be uncomfortable; it's fine for leafing through a magazine with a cup of coffee or a glass of *mirto* in your hand. As long as you don't want to seek isolation by retiring to your own room, the couch on the mezzanine remains one of the best places to do some reading; it's a particular favorite with the kids, who here can idly browse through books, play games and chat, without having to mingle with the grownups.

At times I delude myself into imagining the romance of spending part of the day reading in the shade cast by the branches of the shrubs and trees of the surrounding Mediterranean maquis, in the sort of eighteenth-century situation you find in the tiny glades of the Villa Borghese in Rome or in London's Green Park: among the junipers, under the holm oaks, in the thicket along the path next to the portico. But it is just that, a delusion, a nice idea and that's all, for it is something that everyone thinks about and no one does. When we go down to the sea, out of habit and as a precaution, we tend to slip a book or something else on paper into the towel; but either there's too much wind, or the pages reflect too much light in the sunshine, or we are distracted by the crashing of the waves, or we can't find the right position, and in the end no one ever reads. There is no need for any other places to read than the almost ideal ones that are already there in the house.

The holiday house is a type of building that answers
to many different philosophies. It is not just a place disconnected
from the world outside and apparently devoid of architectural
problems, where you go for a break a few weeks a year; there are as
many holiday houses as there are ideas of what a holiday should
be. A house and a villa built by two Milanese architects a few years
and kilometers apart are very different from one another; each has
its own language and spirit, materials, and idea of life. In short its
own philosophy. Casa Zanuso at Barca Bruciata in Cannigione was
designed by Marco Zanuso for his brother Michele and sister-in-
law Berty in 1963. Villa La Cerva at Porto Cervo was designed by
Luigi Vietti for himself in 1968.

	Casa Zanuso		Villa Vietti
short construction	–	long construction
open and sunny	–	cave-like
one drawing	–	multiple drawings
cheap	–	expensive
monastic	–	opulent
one material	–	many materials
sculptural	–	picturesque
without details	–	many details
spartan	–	luxurious
existential	–	worldly
orthogonal	–	freehand
hard	–	soft
tectonic	–	decorated
visible	–	invisible
desert	–	tropical

The two houses contrast two ways of being on holiday. Vietti thought that a vacation meant letting oneself be transported into a dreamlike, surreal dimension; his villa is an aquarium, even a kind of Salvador Dalí painting. Zanuso on the other hand thought that being on holiday was not a time for looking outward, but for going deeply into the awareness of oneself. Two points of view that are poles apart ideologically, with no dialogue possible between them. Where nature and the landscape are concerned, Villa Vietti is a ruin in which the peeling plaster reveals the stone beneath, a folly trapped in and devoured by the vegetation (watered on a daily basis) that grows in the beds along the facades and on the inside: plants with brightly colored flowers like hibiscus, plumbago, and bougainvillea. Casa Zanuso instead accepts the semiarid local climate and adapts to it without contemplating a physical and aesthetic transformation of the ecosystem; it makes you feel that water here is a precious commodity, to be conserved and savored. The plans of the two houses are also in strong contrast, even though both are located on a flat plot of land a stone's throw from the sea. One seems to have been designed for aperitifs and to reel in clients, the other as a place to be alone and read a good book.

The plan of Villa Vietti, in the heart of the Costa Smeralda, branches out in many directions, and leaves room to grow farther. There are an external courtyard, a hexagonal entrance, steps everywhere, a sunken living area, an alcove where eight can dine, a green corridor that serves as a conservatory, a skewed portico facing onto the sea; instead of straight walls or right angles there are false wooden beams. The roof slopes in all directions, the windows are almost all different shapes and sizes, the expressionistic chimneys wink at Gaudí. There are four bedrooms of generous size with bathrooms and walk-in closets, but the sea is visible from only one. There is accommodation for four servants. The plan was lovingly drawn in pencil and by hand. Bachisio Bandinu, a Sardinian anthropologist and longstanding critic of the ideology on which the iconography of the Costa Smeralda rests, comments with acid lucidity:

> The roughness of the walls is not that of the *stazzo*; it does not call for more days of work but is a sign of there having been too many: it is a mark of surplus labor. The protruding beam of darkened wood serves to conceal a slender and sturdy line of concrete. Only the power of tourism is able to age a beam of juniper and shorten into the work time of the builder the effect of centuries and centuries of wind, rain and sun. The resemblance between the bent and crooked wall of the *stazzo* and that of the villa is fake: the former is a genetic defect, the second is a demonstration of skill; the former is the product of necessity, the second of free choice. The tourist has chosen the crooked wall because he already has many straight ones.

Facing onto the Gulf of Arzachena, Casa Zanuso on the other hand has the form of a square enclosure, with four rooms, one at each corner, and a cross-shaped patio at the center. It has been

Marco Zanuso, Casa Zanuso, Arzachena.
Photographer Michele Zanuso/Archivio Marco Zanuso Jr.

described metaphorically as a tent, a sheepfold, a fort, a church, a classicizing structure; these analogies can still be discerned but do not affect its identity, which is genuine, free from explicit allusions. The plan, slightly modified over the years, has not lost its radical character and is a marvel. Originally everything was located inside the fort: three bedrooms with washbasins and a living room-kitchen at the corners, and a single bathroom in one of the arms of the cross. Marco Zanuso Jr, homonymous nephew of its designer, recalls: "We spent much of the time outside on the patio, and the view extended to the east through a big and beautiful window opening right onto the sea." To the east, in the direction of the rising sun, a large *tholos* was subsequently added to serve as a living room, while to the west a small *tholos* was added as a bathroom, following a logic of growth by budding, of the kind to be seen in many nuraghes. The holiday here is informal. The carefully contrived original ambiguity between inside and outside, the basis of a whole poetics, has survived. "What really changed things a lot was the arrival around 1970 of electricity, which on the one hand has solved many practical and objective problems, but on the other has meant the loss of something forever."

Near Casa Zanuso, at the opposite end of a long stretch of beach, is another house built in 1962 by another Milanese architect and well-known industrial designer, Vico Magistretti. Casa Arosio is very close to the water and remarkably tiny, not much more than a bungalow. Perhaps Magistretti was inspired by the experimental L-shaped house that Alvar Aalto had built for himself ten years earlier on a lake at Muuratsalo, in Finland. Aalto in those years was popular in Italy, and a major exhibition of his work was held at Palazzo Strozzi in Florence in 1965. The Arosio family have always regarded their refuge as a close relative of a sailboat. "They had a thing about Polynesia, my parents!" says Enrico, the son of the owners. Early photos show the house surrounded by yellow pastures, the landscape of sixty years ago, with no vegetation but grass and not a trace of shade; today a dark pinewood grows around it, making it almost invisible. It is reminiscent of a small white *stazzo*, although its T-shaped plan proves that it is not a work of vernacular architecture. The long side faces onto the foreshore and contains a portico and two bedrooms, each with a bathroom of its own; above the portico there is a third makeshift bedroom, for the kids; behind the portico, in the stem of the T, are the living room with a fireplace and a basic kitchen. The ridge of the roof runs parallel to the water. As soon as you wake up in the morning you walk a few meters, open a little wooden gate that gives onto the beach and dive straight into sea; a few strokes toward the rising sun and then back for coffee. A splendid start to the day. It is a clear and straightforward house, devoid of rhetoric, whose message reduces the philosophy of the seaside holiday to the minimum terms of subsistence.

Both Casa Zanuso and Casa Arosio face onto a beach that in those early years seemed private but today is frequented by many vacationers. Both have few ancillary services and speak of the desire and the courage, on the part of two middle-class families from Milan, to spend a certain period of the year in the wilds. Spartan but not rudimentary, their idea of comfort is one that relates principally to the summer season. In their architectural sensibility, they are houses that pertain to the dawn of critical regionalism; if on the one hand they underline the distance between Milan and Sardinia, on the other they reflect something of the fact that certain tourists already wanted to learn from Sardinia. One is reminded of a movie that Lina Wertmüller made in 1968 on the beaches of the Gulf of Orosei, a hundred or so kilometers south of the Gulf of Arzachena, starring Giancarlo Giannini and Mariangela Melato: *Swept Away by an Unusual Destiny in the Blue Sea of August* is its lengthy, but witty and acutely sarcastic title. The plot tells us something about Italian society. Raffaella Pavone Lanzetti is a wealthy bourgeois blonde on vacation aboard a yacht in the Mediterranean, while Gennarino Carunchio is a bearded communist deckhand from Sicily. The breakdown of an outboard motor leaves the pair stranded on a dinghy in the open sea. Eventually they land on a deserted island; here their social roles are reversed and a passionate love affair ensues, a magnificent waking dream. Returning to civilization, their different social classes separate them; the idealist Gennarino tries to persuade Raffaella to go back to the island with him, but realistically she refuses.

Vico Magistretti, Casa Arosio, Arzachena.
Archivio Vico Magistretti.

Cini Boeri, Casa Boeri, La Maddalena.
© Helenio Barbetta.

A mixture of comfort and adventure can be found in all the tourist architecture of Sardinia. When the level of comfort is low, it's a problem; but when it's too high, it generates another and worse one. If you get the quantity right, comfort magically turns into luxury. In Latin *luxus* means excess, surfeit. Today, in reference to tourism, luxury should signify adventure, but also consideration for the place.

The house that Cini Boeri built for herself at Punta Cannone, in the northern part of the island of La Maddalena, resembles Casa Zanuso in its form, but differs as far as the philosophy of comfort is concerned. Cini Boeri worked in Marco Zanuso's studio until 1963, and so it is certain that before designing her own house in 1967 she had already collaborated on that of the Zanuso family, a project that for her served as a prototype and reference. Casa Boeri has four bedrooms at the four corners, each with its own bathroom and a niche-cum-French window giving onto the sea, just a few meters away. The living room is on multiple levels and performs the same role as the cruciform patio in Casa Zanuso. On the upper side a kitchen serves as an entrance, while on the side of the sea, wind permitting, it is possible to stretch an awning over a small courtyard (closed in the winter with two wooden doors) to provide a bit of shade. The flat roof was supposed to have been used as a solarium like the one at Villa Malaparte on Capri, but in the end a deck and a jetty on the water were constructed for this purpose. The inhabitants of La Maddalena call it the bunker, with its dark gray color and slanting walls almost devoid of windows; the reference to the military forts of the archipelago and to Guardiavecchia (the radar base for the control of navigation in the Strait of Bonifacio) is literal. If Casa Zanuso is steeped in a sense of the sacred, Casa Boeri is infused with comfort. Inside, it is a gem of interior design, a masterly three-dimensional jigsaw puzzle. Steps, ledges, shelves, closets, bunkbeds, lofts, drawers, and hideaways interlock to create something elegant that is also an enchanting and surprising inner world. It is an ergonomic refuge, in which you have to move with circumspection and discretion. In pushing practicality to a level of perfection, Cini Boeri succeeded in getting comfort to coincide with luxury.

In the 1960s, in a limited area in the north of Sardinia, four architects from mainland Italy—the Milanese Luigi Vietti, Marco Zanuso, Vico Magistretti, and Cini Boeri—represented four different ideas of the holiday. In those same years the Partito Sardo d'Azione/Partidu Sardu regarded all newcomers as "colonialists," and the Marxist Milanese publisher Giangiacomo Feltrinelli, lending his support, went so far as to describe Sardinia as "the Cuba of the Mediterranean." I remember angry teachers from Palau picketing the rocks in front of my house with their students for hours, brandishing placards declaring "Sardinia for the Sardinians." At the time, each of the four architects had a practice in Milan, a big city; with the sole exception of Vietti, they were not looking for work in Sardinia, and still less did they consider the possibility of coming to live there. Of the four, Vietti was the oldest, born in 1903; he had begun his professional career under Fascism and built his showcase at Porto Cervo at the age of almost sixty; he died in Milan in 1998. Vico Magistretti was born in 1920 in Milan, where he died in 2006, and was just over forty when he built Casa Arosio; he was a versatile man and a designer in the functionalist mold, a sworn enemy of all vulgarity; he loved London and England. Marco Zanuso (1916–2001), also an architect and designer, graduated in 1939 and over the course of his life focused in particular on themes linked to industrialization of the building trade and technology, but in Sardinia ended up creating an archaic structure along Kahnian lines, at the age of forty-five. Cini Boeri (1924–2020) had just turned forty when she built her house on La Maddalena.

All four houses are now over fifty years old and are still owned by the heirs of the original owners, which means they have never been sold and that they have always been looked after as works of architecture. By the sixties Vietti had already repudiated his links with rationalism and had no scruples about messing about with the most diverse materials and styles, in an effort to invent for himself an improbable neo-vernacular style. In contrast Boeri, Zanuso, and Magistretti remained stalwart in their commitment to modernism, which meant they had to deal with the usual kinds of technical problems faced by all colonizers, finding the right middle way between the purity of their enlightened vision and the local way of doing things: "Where can I find and buy beautiful tiles?" "Do you by any chance know someone in the area who is able to build a flat roof that doesn't leak?" "Where will the contractor get the sand to make the concrete?" "Let's hope that the aluminum doors and windows will last so near the sea!" "Do we really need to cut into the rock to make an undercroft, even though we only plan to come in the summer?" "Please let's try to save those myrtle and rosemary bushes!" "Here's the list of the things I'm going to get my trusted artisans in Milan to make, and that I'll have sent to you as soon as possible …"

The Mediterranean scrub around the house varies little from season to season. It is monotonous and fairly neutral compared with other ecosystems, and it is impossible to walk through. The vegetation is almost always the same dull and grayish shade of green, and from a certain distance looks like moss. The principal plants (juniper, holm oak, myrtle, wild olive, arbutus, rockrose, spurge, broom), bearing either leaves or needles, are almost all evergreen. Sardinia is gradually returning to its natural state as a forest, one made up chiefly of holm oaks. This has taken little more than a generation; the speed of the change is astonishing, hardly more than the blink of an eye. The few flowers of the shrubs that make up the scrub last only a short time, and the berries and fruits are small and not very visible; the only exception is the arbutus, or strawberry tree, whose three seasonal colors (white, red, green) have made it a national symbol of Italy. The parched and yellow landscapes of the past have almost completely vanished, and there is hardly any arid land left; the cows, sheep, and goats, the peasants, shepherds, wildflowers, and low dry stone walls marking property boundaries that once embroidered the landscape have disappeared too. Along the watercourses where there is moisture and that good smell of decay there are eucalyptuses (foreign) and oleanders and figs (native). In the little gardens and the parking lots, on the balconies and in the flowerbeds, the tourists expect to see suburban scenes with bougainvillea, cacti, and lavender, as well as lemon trees in terracotta pots. Along the main roads the nurseries sell exotic plants from other parts of the world with a Mediterranean climate: California, Chile, South Africa, Australia. Most people expect to be supplied with water in large quantities at low cost and they are, thanks to the reservoirs that fill some of the inland valleys. The small private villas are surrounded by lawns so smooth and perfect they look like miniature golf courses, tended by professional gardeners. At Arzachena and Luogosanto today there are vineyards producing good white and red wines, something that did not exist before.

Many people cannot tell the difference between nature and agriculture; they ought to read *Works and Days* by the Greek poet Hesiod and *De re rustica* by the Roman writer Marcus Terentius Varro, two books that explain the effort that goes into the transformation of the world. My parents tried to create a small vegetable garden, and this represented yet another challenge for them, an attempt to prove to themselves that they were self-sufficient, that they had little need for others: if Sardinia's economy was one of subsistence, that of the Brandolini family could be too. As well as living in isolation and going fishing every day, we could grow our own vegetables. Initially my father, who had a degree in agricultural science, chose to lay out the vegetable garden on a piece of flat ground sheltered by rocks, measuring about ten square meters, above the cesspool and just to the right of the house; a fair number of sacks of fertile topsoil were brought in: its black color was completely different from that of the pale and sandy soil found in the area. Cut stones were used to build a mini-enclosure of around four square meters, and Pietro Filigheddu (husband of Rosa, our housekeeper) was given the job of sowing tomatoes, peppers, zucchini, and eggplant, along with a few herbs, in the spring. The experiment failed because the soil turned out not to be very fertile, and as everyone was hungry demand greatly exceeded supply. It was impossible to produce five kilos of tomatoes and two kilos of zucchini and eggplant a day, and water was already scarce. So my father found a new location for the vegetable garden, on a larger plot of land with better soil, but farther from the house: a valley near the gate running along the boundary of the property, above the well that had been dug to provide water. Optimistically, we thought that here, from June to August, we would be able to cultivate vegetables in abundance. But this second project also failed, or rather faded over time. Like all vegetable gardens it required work, patience, and regularity, and moreover there was no synchrony between when the fruit and vegetables were ripe and when they were needed. The garden stopped being fun and became a responsibility, and this shift altered its original spirit. Better—we all thought—was the reliable produce store in Palau, run by a man called Scarpa; to hell with self-sufficiency and grow-your-own.

A few years ago a Milanese real estate agent asked me how much it cost to keep the two hectares of garden around the house in such good order. I told him that unfortunately he was mistaken because there was no garden but thanked him anyway for the implicit compliment. Later a Ligurian agronomist told me I ought to take a bit more care of the scrub, at least gather up the dry leaves and branches and do a bit of pruning, and that if I wished he would send someone trustworthy to do the minimum necessary. I replied that in my view when you start trying to keep vegetation in order the job is never-ending, and that I didn't want to embark on such an enterprise, in part because it was something that would have to be repeated every year. Last year a landscape architect from Zurich told me that the wilderness is itself a garden, and I am fully in agreement with this typically Swiss concept.

In reality, over the course of the first ten years of the house's life, let's say up until the end of the seventies, we too went to a lot of trouble eliminating many of the plants that we considered of little value. We pruned masses of low shrubs, cutting the dry branches so that they would grow with more vigor and become trees five meters tall, as beautiful and large as their species was supposed to be. Around five o'clock, following the afternoon nap and when the heat started to ease off, my father, my brother, and I, joined by any willing guests, would set to work armed with saws, shears, hatchets, spades, shovels, and picks and sweating profusely. We disappeared into the scrub we had decided to turn into a pleasant grove with the idea that in the future we would be able to sit there and read a good Simenon novel. We ended up covered in scratches, cuts, and bruises, but even with blisters on our hands we were content. The practical results of our efforts were variable; in some areas the plants benefited and from that moment on grew in exactly the way we had imagined; but in other places the plants, once thinned out, were invaded by brambles and sadly died out over the years. We eventually realized that keeping the Mediterranean scrub in a state of apparent order was a Sisyphean task, and not worth the effort. One day we even decided to make an attempt at embellishment, importing new species of tree (olives, eucalyptuses, stone pines) and hoping they would take in the positions we had selected, but it was a flop. Today you can't tell the difference between where we pruned and where we did nothing. Should we be disappointed or satisfied? The wild and impassable Mediterranean maquis has come close to the house and casts flickering shadows on the pink walls; every so often we cut off some branches or fill a few black plastic garbage bags with dry leaves, if only to reduce the risk of fires, but in doing so it feels as if we are abusing nature. In his 1929 novel *Station at the Horizon*, Erich Maria Remarque has the charming Lilian Dunquerke say of her park on the Côte d'Azur: "Yes, the park has grown wild, so they keep telling me. But I can't make up my mind to deprive it of its freedom. Its gods are forbearing and silent. Their death should not be disturbed by the gardeners' shears. Indeed, I would be happier if the vegetation slowly covered them up ..."

The Mediterranean maquis is a forest in miniature; whether low or high, it forms a barrier of plants that mingle and entwine as if they were copulating. There are no ways out, and at times it is so thick that to move forward you have to go backward, ass first. The ground is full of little stones, hollows, holes, and branches that take forever to decompose. You hear the twittering of birds and the rustling of insects, small mammals, and reptiles, but you don't see them. You can barely feel the wind, but the scents and odors are very strong. The maquis is democratic, because it does not allow one species of plant to prevail over the others. But some plants have always been closer to our hearts than others. We've always revered the junipers, symbols of beauty and strength; we like the hardness and scent of their resinous wood, their fibrous bark, the symmetrical arrangement of their branches, their hard fruit which you can use as marbles or to play tricks. You need to think twice, before pruning or cutting down a juniper! Up at the parking place, guests were greeted for many years by the skeleton of a juniper, composed of a vertical trunk a couple of meters tall that halfway up split into three thick branches, onto which a plate bearing the name "Brandolini" in cursive script was fixed with two large iron screws. The trunk was first a reddish color, then brown, and in the end silver. It was at once tree, column, sign, totem, idol, coat of arms, and crucifix; originally I think it had been where the house was then built; in the end the skeleton that was left fell over, partly because its base had become unstable and partly because the water tank next to it was enlarged.

Another mythical juniper was the one that grew right in front of the house, where it was exposed to the full force of the Maestrale. For this reason it was and should have remained low, so as to protect itself from the wind with its dry branches, perhaps not very attractive but necessary all the same. We didn't know this, and every year we cut off the dry bits because they blocked our view of the rocky and watery panorama; in our ignorance we thought that we could turn the juniper bush into a tree. In the end we realized that we had killed it, as a result of wanting it to be different from what it was. For a while we used it as a structure on which to hang our towels to dry, then we cut it down. All that remains today is its stump, ineradicable.

There is a juniper that we have never touched and that we just admire. Exposed completely to the wind and bent back on itself like a rickety old man, it grows in the fissure of a steep granite face; having reached a height of about sixty centimeters, it is inconceivable that it will get any taller. It is in excellent health and according to my two agronomist and landscape designer friends is a rare example of a natural bonsai that could be hundreds of years old and the most precious plant on the property. Should we give it a name? Wrinkled and clinging to the rock like a climber, ascetic, and solitary, all it needs to survive is the seasonal water that accumulates in the fissure and the minerals contained in the grains of granite. It really is satisfied with little or nothing.

Lower down, just above the natural pool, there are two imposing junipers, low and branching out horizontally, whose proportions and aura are absolutely Japanese. The contrast in scale with the bonsai is surprising: how can it be the same plant? By chance, they were spared our pruning frenzy of fifty years ago, perhaps because we thought they fulfilled our aesthetic expectations from the outset. Since then, they have spread out considerably without growing much in height, and today present an appearance much in harmony with the nearby masses of granite. They don't care about the wind, protected as they are by their dry branches which look like lace, as in the exquisite woodcuts of Utagawa Hiroshige. They have grown so much that they block the little path that used to connect the house to the pool.

Although many consider it immoral for the nurseries to import exotic plants, Sardinia remains for us an exotic island. "It's so far away from Italy." You think this every time when, after a nocturnal voyage aboard the ferry from Genoa or Livorno, you see its purplish gray mountains standing out clearly on the horizon. Here the sea is a different blue. You begin to feel its winds and smell its special odors. The distance from Italy is also evident from the way the plants here grow just as they please, heedless of the presence of human beings, in well-chosen and slightly different places every year, assuming forms that seem to us a bit absurd, eccentricities of nature. Each micro-landscape is no more than a few hundred square meters in size and has its own micro-flora.

The sour fig (*Carpobrotus acinaciformis*), known as the *erba di Garibaldi* in Italian, is a perennial succulent originating from the Cape Province in South Africa and now naturalized all over the Mediterranean basin. Its fruits are edible and its decorative and mostly purple flowers are used to make a sour jam; its long stems creep over the rocks and sand, and are often found dried up, ready to crumble into dust; its leaves have a triangular section. *Helichrysum italicum* (in Greek, *helios* means sun and *chrysos* gold), sometimes called the curry plant, is at ease in front of the house; it looks like a large tuft of grass, although it is classified as a shrub. It grows in poor and immature soils near the coast, on sites that may once have been covered with scrub. It is strongly scented and its many medicinal properties have been known since ancient times: it is used to treat respiratory, rheumatic, and hepatic diseases and as a remedy for headaches. The flowers retain their color when dried and are used in closets and wardrobes. In the summer we regularly come across isolated stalks of a plant from the great *Allium* family: a smooth stem about a meter in height, a ball-shaped flower and a bulb that smells more like onion than garlic; I don't know if it is edible. Alongside the dirt road grow swathes of wild fennel (*Foeniculum vulgare*), sometimes over two meters tall; its roots, flowers, and fruits (which are not, strictly speaking, seeds) are extensively used in cooking, for example in the Sicilian dish of pasta with sardines; its infusions relieve disturbances of the bowel; in large quantities it is hallucinogenic, and it is said that its flavor alters the taste of wine. The white asphodel (*Asphodelus albus, s'iscraria* in Sardinian) was legendary in antiquity (in ancient Greece it was considered the plant of the dead), a reputation it has retained in modern times (in the first volume of the Harry Potter series it is used to make a "Draught of Living Death"). It is a herbaceous species that produces a bare stem from which blooms a spike of white flowers whose ethereal petals have a dark stripe running down the middle. Out of respect for and in memory of our forebears, we could light a fire with its stalks, use its root in cooking, weave its stems to make big baskets (once in Sardinia these baskets were a fundamental part of the bride's trousseau before marriage); its leaves on the ground regenerate continually, a fact much appreciated by goats that in exchange allow the seeds—which they love—to remain active after passing through their digestive systems.

9 *Rocks*

No imagination is needed to recognize fragments of reality in the forms of the rocks in front of the house. The fact that everyone sees different and contradictory things in them doesn't mean they are not true figures, perhaps truer even than reality itself. The rocks and stones are animals, plants, fruits, ornaments, musical instruments, toys, means of transport, industrial components, bits and pieces of who knows what. They are apocryphal works of Jean Arp, Giuseppe Capogrossi, Salvador Dalí, Max Ernst, Barbara Hepworth, Le Corbusier, Henry Moore, and Giuseppe Santomaso, among many other possible artists. Here geology has portrayed the world we human beings have created and in which we live. It took me years to understand this, and now I am convinced that this is really how we perceive the things around us. Gavino Ledda, in his autobiography *Padre Padrone: L'educazione di un pastore* (published in 1975, and subsequently translated into

Aerial view of the house with surrounding rocks.
© Waterfront Italy/John Bracco.

forty languages), relates how something similar happened to him as a child:

> "Every tree, every boulder, every sheep, every point or configuration of the land in 'our' field or the surrounding mountains and on the horizon, I had given a pet name which I kept secretly hidden in that silence with which, in a way, everything spoke to me and for me was alive. ... I likened the whole of reality, from trees to mountain peaks, from rocks to caves, from sheep to wild beasts, to people or things that I, occasionally, had seen elsewhere."

There are four particular rocks in front of the house that I would like to describe.

Elephant. It is a large sphere, one that would deserve to be mentioned in all books on granite. It is miraculously intact on top, but carved by the wind and the salt water of the sea underneath. It is a cavity in evolution that sleeps and serves as our talisman. Sardinia is full of idols and totems and every town and village has at least one. According to Salvatore Satta, a jurist from Nuoro and author of the autobiographical novel *Il giorno del giudizio* (published posthumously in 1977), it is hope that generates idols, and then the idols that give rise to solitude. You can clearly see that the Elephant has two tusks, a trunk, two eyes, and four sturdy legs pressing against two steep walls of granite that form a V-shaped hollow. One of the two front legs is bent and serves as a balcony, should anyone wish to try to clamber onto its back; so far only one young man has succeeded in doing so, without climbing shoes. Walking on the two rocks that flank it, you notice its powerful muscles, which arch to support its weight, and perceive the agility of this long-lived semi-prehistoric being, which has decided to end its days here in semi-aqueous tranquility. Its rump, turned toward the sea, is fascinating too; it is a beautiful backside, firm, gray, and round like Babar's, about ten meters high, rough, and covered with lichen that outlines a geographical map. Although there is little room to swim under its belly, the water is deep enough; suspicious noises come from its body, gargles, perhaps a bit of flatulence. The water produces eddies, echoes, murmurs, burps, and bubbles of sound. From underneath its immense bulk is impressive; the skull, tusks, mouth and trunk all overhang, suspended in midair. The elephant is a vain seducer, conscious of its curves and chiaroscuro effects, and likes to be seen and portrayed from different points of view. But so far no photograph or drawing has truly done it justice.

Netsuke. It is a rock so small and perfect that at the end of every summer I find myself wanting to take it away with me. *Netsukes* are tiny and precious Japanese ornamental toggles that fix small containers or objects to the belt of a kimono (*ne* means root, *tsuke* to attach); they are to an equal extent functional and artistic, objects and sculptures, and possess a spirit that verges on the diabolical, like the granite rocks. They enchant our sight and our touch, and once we get hold of one we cannot stop looking at it and fiddling around with it. Our Netsuke is a three-pointed star, with a diameter of about two meters; it lies at the water's edge, next to where we usually sunbathe. Its base, always wet, sits on a rock just beneath the surface; the rest emerges about fifty centimeters out of the water at the average height of the tide. You can climb onto the Netsuke from the shore with a single step; it will hold two people at most, standing or seated, as there's not much room. If a wave breaks it will be submerged for a few seconds, but then, since its highest point is at its center, the water immediately flows off in all directions and it dries. No pools are formed on its surface, unlike on the top of all the others. I ask myself why I like this rock so much. Perhaps because it is so discreet, perhaps because its form and its position are so perfectly suited to one another. Many people don't see anything special in it, and don't even notice its presence.

Pyramid. It is a rock of hypnotic appearance next to the house, and its geometry must once have been that of a sort of Platonic solid, probably an irregular octahedron; but then the wind must have turned, deformed, masked, and eroded it, smoothing and blunting the edges. Its geometry has grown enigmatic and shifty, too complicated to comprehend. The more you look at it, the less you understand it, like some seashells. The Pyramid is a monolith that rests on the ground in apparently precarious balance; it certainly can't move, it's far too heavy. For the kids it's a second

Pastel drawing of the Netsuke by the author, 1970.
Archive Sebastiano Brandolini.

house, at once a refuge, hideout, observation post, and gym. You walk past it when you go down to the sea, and you place a hand on it to keep steady, just a caress. In its side an oval hole as big as a head (with a smaller one underneath the size of a fist) serves as a secret compartment for the house key while we're down at the sea; in winter birds nest inside. It is possible to creep under it on your hands and knees; you enter apprehensively on one side and come out with satisfaction on the other. Above, there is a mini-mountaineering route: ascent on the south face, descent on the north face, difference in height, four meters. You start by climbing two steps that lead to a flattish cavity about the size of a bed, where the rainwater collects in the winter; from here you grab hold of a handle, clamber over a balcony, and reach a watershed crest where it's wiser not to stand, especially on windy days; you descend carefully down a forty-five-degree slope (this is where the bonsai juniper is located) that offers good grips for the hands and holds for the feet; the last gap of a meter is overcome with a leap.

Dinosaur. A postcard bought at the tobacconist's in the port of Palau opened our eyes: next to the house lived a dinosaur. Before, no one had noticed that the rock looked like a prehistoric animal; indeed no one had even given that rock a name, referring to it just as "the rock with holes in it." No matter, people can see in these stones whatsoever they wish. None of the rocks described so far brazenly challenges the law of gravity, as they are all embedded in the ground and have clear points of support: the Elephant is an eroded sphere balanced on three of its four legs, the Netsuke a mass of eight tons stranded on the foreshore, the Pyramid a geometric solid. But the Dinosaur really does challenge the law of gravity, so much so that one day I'd like to talk to a structural engineer who can tell me why it hasn't yet collapsed. Is there an equation that can explain why the eye says one thing and physics another? The shape of the Dinosaur is that of a tongue/hand cantilevered out over the water; you can walk on its back and swim under its palm. Each of its three fingers contains a hole in a different stage of erosion: the first hole looks like a bean and is perfectly smooth and well-shaped; the second is squarer in form and a large crack on one side makes it look as if it is about to break off, although it has always been like that; the third hole—we can guess—was once

Dinosaur—postcard.
Archive Sebastiano Brandolini.

there but no longer exists, as a collapse has turned it into a recess. To reach the Dinosaur from land, it is necessary to climb and make a few athletic leaps: descend into the steep V-shaped hollow where the Elephant is located, clamber over some slippery little rocks flush with the surface of the water, ascend the opposite side where the granite is fissured and rotten and makes a sound like plaster, stop for a few moments on a crest of pinkish-brown granite that runs down to the water, descend a face with a slope of about thirty degrees, and finally pluck up enough courage to do a running jump onto the back of what in all its dreamlike appearance looks like a dinosaur. From its back, I have always wanted to dive through one of the holes into the water. Swimming or floating under the Dinosaur and stroking the erotic curves and folds of its belly can be considered an experience of body art. In the afternoon, you see the sky framed by the holes as you swim, while beams of sunlight are refracted in the water; you can hear the bass notes of the echo made by the waves as they slam against the lower surface of this cavernous rock. You have to be careful not to bang your head on it, for the waves lift you up and the rock slopes downward. In the meantime your feet caress the Neptune grass, *Posidonia oceanica*, that grows on the seabed a couple of meters below.

The natural swimming pool (Piscina) is the stage that links these four rocks together at sea level, creating visual triangulations, an alcove where the sea has succeeded in breaking through the wall of granite. From the practical viewpoint, it was for years our exclusive harbor, the workspace in which to moor and keep the rubber dinghy, sailboat, and rowboat; there was also a triangular deck of tarred wood on which to clean the fishing nets, store the jerry cans of gasoline, gut the fish, and keep the lobster pots. Today the Piscina has ceased to be a workspace and has resumed its role as a laboratory of nature, there to intrigue and confuse our minds. In it little children splash water with their hands and feet before learning to swim, just like the fingerlings of mullet and sardine that do their training here before venturing into the open sea. Everything is in miniature: two islets, two shoals, a little beach, a diving board, a small wall to climb, a channel just two meters wide, and two old rings of rusty iron to which the boats used to be tied. The water, never completely still, enters and exits from two points, one to the east and one to the west. The waves produced by the micro-currents and the gusts of wind hypnotize and anesthetize us and we can watch them for hours without getting bored. The seabed, on which we can walk by letting ourselves sink a little, conveys messages that change with the temperature of the air, as this seems to influence its density. When there is little current, the water looks like glass in the daytime and oil at night. When the current swirls, everything overflows and goes in all directions: a turbulence, a moment of psychedelic madness, beyond our mental capacities of understanding and prediction. All this happens in a limited space, because the Piscina measures scarcely one hundred square meters. It doesn't take an ocean, storm, or cascade to throw everything into confusion, but far less.

Speaking of how smooth these rocks are is once again like talking about something that lacks substance. It's like speaking of the wind, whose presence is the consequence of its immateriality. The smoothness of granite is in reality the effect of its being worn away. Here the passage of time portrays itself. The eyes grasp the overall shapes, while the feet feel the grains that form the texture of the granite. The only thing that holds together these two scales, that of sight and that of touch, is sensuality. Concavity and convexity play a complex game that thwarts any reasoning based on the analytical and synthetic rules of descriptive geometry. What is it that has made the rocks here so different from the ones along other stretches of the coast? What really happened here? Was it the result of the chemical composition of the granite, the temperature, and the pressure at which it was formed? Or is the wind really the main agent at work? What help can the exact sciences offer us in understanding why the Elephant, the Pyramid, the Netsuke, and the Dinosaur are all here, keeping each other company? Why is the granite so erotic, and why are the hollows so soft and why do the undulations so closely resemble the forms of a curvaceous body? The rocks crowd around us and after putting us in a daze, threaten us; from every angle they challenge our reason, intuition, and comprehension. The more we look at them, the less we understand them. Sight and touch, senses that normally work together to give us a comprehensive and comprehensible vision of the world, do not tally here. Something invites us to lie on the rocks for hours and fall into a light state of trance. Adhering to the curves of the rocks, we massage every curve of our body: the nape of the neck, shoulders, back, buttocks, thighs, calves, heels, and feet. But we never assume positions in which we could let ourselves go completely. In the end, the foot is the sensor which knows these rocks best, and which guides our posture, our balance, and the direction of our gaze.

From a hard-to-find balcony above the house, the Elephant, the Netsuke, and the Pyramid are visible together: three soloists in a symphony orchestra. The granite of the balcony is more or less flat, and you could even lie down and take a nap, except that the sun is right overhead. In the spring tiny succulents, as red as coral, grow in its cracks, and large junipers resistant to the wind have taken possession of more space than the goats allowed them sixty years ago. All that can be seen of the house just below is a corner of the roof. I think: perhaps it should never have been built in a place like this ... Perhaps my parents, in their innocence and enthusiasm, have disfigured the environment ... Perhaps our three rocks are the seracs, crevasses, and pinnacles of the front of a granite glacier ... I look: the glacier starts from the Orso, where its catchment basin is located ... Three tongues of granite radiate down from it to the north ... It is on one of these tongues that the house was built ... The stones I like most are among those most exposed to erosion due to the current rise in sea level ... So they are the ones that are going to disappear first ... Other spectacular rocks will arrive ... It will be the turn of the ones in the second and third row. I imagine: the stones that loom over the parking place are in reality pieces of a serac of one of the tongues of granite that are sliding slowly toward the sea, at an immeasurably slow pace ... When it fissures new masses will be formed that will break free from their base ... And could in their turn roll down ... All of this vaguely resembles an apocalypse, a nightmare.

Some boulders have detached from their base and are now free from static constraints. The Netsuke, once much bigger, is soon going to disappear, however much it resists, turning from igneous rock into sedimentary rock. The Elephant has stopped there, delicately wedged into that V-shaped fissure, after rolling down in a landslide caused by an earthquake, in the long-ago Silurian period. A geologist friend once told me that things did not go the way I have imagined them, but not even he knows exactly how it all happened. Erosion has not yet detached the Dinosaur from the tectonic plate underneath, otherwise its incredible leap into the void could not be explained. The real animals we see searching for the little fresh water available among the rocks and plants are playing some kind of abstruse and illusory game. Something makes the landscape look like a diorama, summoning up a memory of life rather than life itself. Initially you have the illusion that the surrounding scenery is breathing and alive, and then this gives way to the illusion that it is immobile and dead. This twofold misapprehension puts us in a daze, and determines the tragic nature of the house. Our mind, befuddled as if it has just woken from a dream, is unable to reconstruct and recall, and still less to decide whether it was a good dream or a bad dream. The shadows that the sun redraws every instant on the rocks describe a movement so slow and imperceptible that you wonder whether they can really be considered to move at all. It's a slowness reminiscent of the video art of Bill Viola, whose works are so magnetic and hypnotic that they could run in a loop forever. It is a slowness that changes the meaning of things.

The precarity of the chaos that unfolds before our eyes becomes clear when we look at a half-hidden composition of granite rocks just a few meters from the house. It is a composition in an absurd position, one that with a little shove would collapse and roll down onto the house. How did these three pieces of granite, each weighing around a ton, reach their current state of unstable equilibrium? What will happen to them in the coming years? In the end, is a breath of wind or a tremor going to destroy that balance? In the meantime, a gray holm oak, grown above them, provides a protective umbrella. The composition is set in a sloping face, standing on a bit of level ground just a meter square. One roundish spheroid has come to rest here; between this spheroid and the rock face rests an inclined slab, which acts as a strut; between this strut and the sloping face lies another slab, this time horizontal. Taken individually, each of these three granite boulders—one a rough sphere, one an inclined slab, one a horizontal slab—is unstable, but together they form a rigid structure, a sort of dolmen. Air passes through the gaps that separate them. Chance must have been the architect of this little miracle of natural engineering. But what is chance really? It is the infinite number of possibilities that things could have turned out differently. Our eye considers and reflects: everything here is the fruit of chance.

Near the house, one of the three tongues of granite forks; each fork is composed of thousands of boulders jumbled one on top of the other; some of the boulders are still anchored at the base, others are already free. They are of the most varied dimensions and walking on them is tiring, because you are continually going up and down and there are no visual references; but they're not slippery and you feel sure on your feet. If we were at high altitude, brushstrokes of red paint would indicate the best route to follow. Between Casa Brandolini and its neighbor, Casa Paccagnella, there is a frighteningly large free mass of rock, precariously balanced about thirty meters above the sea; instinctively you choose not to swim underneath, just in case it should start to roll at that very moment. At its base there is a scattering of sand (grains of feldspar, quartz, and mica), reflecting the incessant process of erosion.

If you continue along the same path that descends from the parking area, you arrive at the sea. The path forks at the Pyramid; if you go right you come to the artificial solarium. A narrow passage between two rocks forces you to squeeze through sideways, holding in your belly; there are also overgrown branches of juniper to dodge. The path descends for about fifteen steps; on the left, sour fig has long been trying to take root on a granite wall, with mixed results; on the right there is a maquette of Henry Moore's 1952 sculpture *King and Queen*. This space, almost flush with the water, floods at spring tide (when the difference between high and low tide reaches its maximum, as the sun, moon, and earth come into line), and then the water runs off into the numerous cracks. It was here that my parents decided to build a solarium (in Latin *solarium* means a sundial), in the lee of the west wind, to supplement the one in front of the house. Before there were just small rocks and pools in this place. The person who did this work without using cement, in the manner of the nuraghes, was Giovanni Bonannini. Patiently, over the course of a winter, every morning that the weather permitted Bonannini rowed his wooden *gozzo* from Palau (trolling two or three lines behind him) and, arriving at Porto Ulisse, moored it in the Piscina and set serenely to work, humming to himself. If the wind rose over the course of the day, he would return to Palau in the evening on foot. Next to the solarium stand two truncated masses of rock, from which he cut and squared the pieces of granite needed for his work, fruit of an ancient knowhow. He did it all, including the steps of the path, by himself, with his rough hands and his simple tools: levers, wedges, sledgehammers, spikes, and pickaxes. We were left gaping when we once watched him at work. To split a stone weighing several hundred kilos, he first thought about what shape the piece he needed ought to be, and then delivered a series of sharp blows with the sledgehammer at a distance of sixty centimeters from the point at which he wanted it to break; once it broke he rough-hewed the stone, trimming it at the sides and turning it into a piece that fitted precisely into the jigsaw puzzle. "But how does he do it?" we asked ourselves in amazement, unaware that the granite concealed secrets and had a life of its own.

If instead you turn left at the Pyramid, you come to the natural solarium, about fifty meters away. As smooth as the teak deck of a Swan, my parents had already noticed it in 1964 on their first visit, and my mother, impulsive as always, had wanted to climb onto it, but had been discouraged from doing so. Friends ask me again and again: "But have the rocks changed over the years?" And my answer is always: "No, they're still the same!" The best way to go down is to take off slippers, sabots, sandals, or thongs and proceed barefoot; the grip of your feet on the rough granite will be excellent, it doesn't hurt and gives you a feeling of security and pleasure. It is necessary, however, to take care and trust in your sense of balance, for the descent is a bit dangerous. Once a lady from the city felt dizzy and slipped from a height of about four meters into the Piscina below, where the water is fifty centimeters deep; she took fright and came away with some scratches, but at least she had a story to tell when she got back to the mainland. Barefoot then, we descend with small steps along a ridge that is narrow at just one point, with the Piscina on the left and round boulders of large size piled up on the right, competing for the available space. Perhaps it is due to the wind that these stones have reached the condition of stability we so admire today. For each boulder we have found a function. On the first, easy to climb even in the dark, we can lie down to gaze at the fixed and falling stars; in the second, hollowed out to form a cave, we can place towel, goggles, fins, and mask; the third serves as a convenient shortcut linking the two solaria; from the last rock, in direct contact with the water, it is possible to try to catch a few fish with hook and line, using the little snails and limpets found on the foreshore as bait. It takes three more leaps (one up, one down, and another up again) to cross two fissures in which the sea boils and reach the natural solarium. On these very rocks in 1967, Henry Clarke portrayed the American actress and model Marisa Berenson, then only twenty, for *Vogue*; in the evening honey-light she wore only some light pink silk lingerie and a complex algae-decoration on her head as our white cat, Biancaneve, sitting nearby, posed in an Egyptian fashion; all details which make her resemble a novel Artemis, ready to strike. On Sundays out of season the two solaria are occupied by fishermen, who mount their long rods there.

> Some Italian friends drop by, with an American acquaintance, about ten years younger than me. It is him speaking.
> —"My mother knew your parents. I came to these rocks as a boy. We have already met. I have photographs! If you like I'll send them to you."
> —"Really? Don't worry about sending me the photographs. It must have been almost fifty years ago! A lot of water has flowed under the bridge since the last time you were here."
> —"Not at all! My mother died three years ago. I came back by myself two years ago, in February, without telling anyone."
> —"I'm sorry, but I don't know what you're talking about."
> —"I came back because in her will my mother expressed the desire for her ashes to be thrown into the sea from these rocks, from the very point where we are now. And that's what I did."

Marisa Berenson posing on the rocks in 1967.
Photographer: Henry Clarke/*Vogue*.

Few architects have been as articulate in their reasoning on the question of inserting architecture into a natural landscape as Alberto Ponis. The landscapes in which he worked in the north of Sardinia, namely Punta Sardegna and Costa Paradiso, were for him places to develop his distinctive ideas and put them to the test. Born in Genoa, Ponis first came to Palau via London in 1963 at the age of thirty. He has spent practically all of his life there since. Straightaway he realized that it was a place where you had to build gracefully, even if he also recognized that without architecture the landscape remains mute. He understood that the only possible way to construct was by designing buildings that would truly be part of that landscape; buildings that blend but do not try to hide in it, for he was aware that the game architecture plays with respect to camouflage is both delicate and dangerous. Many of his houses are sculptures with a special form and a complex and expressive geometry. He takes enormous care over their positioning, to the point of making them almost disappear. He studies, assimilates, digests, and reinvents a world made up of rocks, paths, and *stazzi*, and he does it without caricature and without nostalgia for a past that is vanishing. He exalts the Sardinian landscape as it was before the arrival of mass tourism. He has not worked on the Costa Smeralda.

In his semi-autobiographic volume *Storie di case e ambiente*, Ponis tells the stories of sixteen of his private houses, juggling various points of view: that of the landscape, that of architecture, and that of the psychological relationship between architect and client. These are matters that architects usually keep to themselves, the unspoken thoughts of the trade. Ponis explains just how meticulous and delicate is the surgical operation he carries out on nature. He considers the Mediterranean scrub to be on a par with a Japanese garden, made up of an infinity of details, microscopic points of observation and changes of level. He speaks of the importance of the path leading to a house and its ability to create the right psychological distance between the world we leave behind and that of a vacation home. He talks about how the first ideas put forward by clients are usually banal and predictable, and how as the project proceeds it is increasingly the complications that determine the necessary choices of form, choices that need to be made with courage. The houses described in the book, though distinct in their location and client, are all connected by a style of vacation at odds with the conventional idea of property development in those years; a kind of vacation with no frills rooted in principles of necessity rather than those of pleasure, utilitarian but generous, where solid physicality always prevails over appearances and illusions.

Some of his houses look like masses of granite and are at once visible and invisible. The same questions apply to them as the ones we asked ourselves with respect to the Orso, the great rock-cavern in the vicinity of Palau: can you actually see the Orso or can't you? Is it big or is it small? Is it hiding or does it want to frighten us? Ponis thinks of his houses as the missing pieces of a painting or a mosaic in which a multiplicity of forms are jumbled together and blend into one another. In his paintings his houses are elements of the landscape, pseudo-rocks that are part of the local geology and

Alberto Ponis, on the roof of the Casa Martinez, Punta Sardegna, 1967.
Archive Alberto Ponis.

Alberto Ponis, Studio di Yasmin, Palau.
Photographer Massimo Molinari / Archive Sebastiano Brandolini.

topography. In some houses (for example Casa Martinez at Punta Sardegna from 1967, or Casa Schachter at Costa Paradiso from 1996), he has preserved large granite boulders and put them on display, exploiting their presence for decorative purposes and as a *memento terrae*, to remind himself and others that in the geography of Sardinia something has always preceded the construction of a building, and that this is the *genius loci*. At times he incorporates masses of granite at the base of the outer walls, a technique that has always been the cheapest way of laying foundations. In one of the early chapters of *Padre Padrone*, Gavino Ledda describes a scene in which his father acts as a guide to the minute and detailed geography of the Sardinian countryside:

> The first meal in the hut was followed by the first exploration in the field. This was how pastoral school commenced. On the first reconnaissance he took care to give me lessons on the finding your way in the countryside and the woods. As we walked, he did his best to fix in my mind the characteristic points of the terrain, the oaks that stood out in particular, for their form, their size, their various curves or their blemishes: holes and bumps (*tuvas* and *thoccas*). Or the boulders and bushes (*crastos and barrasòlos*). Drawing on all his experience he helped me to see them as a whole with the other things: painting me a picture of their natural arrangement in order to have fixed points of reference if I should find myself alone or get lost.

There are three houses designed by Ponis I would like to describe, keeping this passage in mind.

Yasmin's Studio is part of the second house my parents built for themselves a few years after the first and at a distance of a few hundred meters, still on the land of Porto Ulisse. It looks more like a mass of granite than a *pinedda*, the hut built of reeds typical of ancient and rural Sardinia, with which it is often compared. The internal space seems to have been created by hollowing out the heart of a boulder, while the outside looks as if it has been sculpted and molded by the wind, turning it into a perfect circle. Along the outer circumference protuberances resembling suction cups contain a bathroom, a storeroom, and a utility room; between them, two recesses serve as an entrance and a secret courtyard, both in the shape of a half-moon. On the side facing the sea, just a few meters away, there is a portico in the form of an arch. The beams of the roof resemble the spokes of a wheel. They meet at the chimney, the geometric center of the circle. The interior is an open-plan space divided into four segments: a kitchen, a living room, a bedroom, and a dining area. As there is no segment where Yasmin could have painted, I have to deduce that the Studio was conceived from the outset as a small structure equipped with everything necessary, *une petite maison*. In Sardinia my mother imitated the Impressionists, working *en plein air*. Its design, the product of a collaboration between Yasmin and Alberto, is the completion of an existing natural situation; the Studio forms a third mass, built adjoining and in addition to, underneath, and alongside, two granite rocks that were already present, roundish in shape, and covered with grayish lichen. In 1975, in what is certainly no coincidence, my mother published a portfolio of five etchings entitled *To be the circle*.

My father ended up selling the second house to a young relative of some friends, encountered by chance at Punta Sardegna.

—"We've just finished building another house, not far from the first, under the Orso."

—"Would you be willing to sell it? We might be interested."

—"Why not? It's big, comfortable, and with a little beach of its own. It also has an annex, a studio for guests, a very special extra."

—"Would you sell both the house and the studio?"

—"Let's talk about it, although Yasmin is not so sure about it. Come and take a look."

—"And why would you want to sell it?"

—"We already have our first house, which we are very fond of and will keep, and that's enough for us."

—"But if I'm not mistaken you have two children."

—"One house is enough for us."

—"Tell me more."

—"It's spacious, designed by Ponis. There are not too many steps, it's less isolated than ours. It has a fine patio sheltered from the west wind, heating, and two large tanks for water. It's near the sea."

—"I'd like to see it, it sounds attractive. My wife and I are looking for something in the area ... Corsica attracts us too ..."

—"Drop by tomorrow. We're leaving the next day."

—"Could you keep a sailboat there too? We have a Grand Soleil."

—"For that I think Palau is better. They're finishing the marina at last, as it should be!"

—"Till tomorrow then. Delighted to have met you. Not bad this Vermentino ..."

Casa Scalesciani at Costa Paradiso is probably the most spectacular of the over two hundred houses designed by Ponis. It is also comparable—at least in terms of its setting—to Villa Malaparte on Capri (1940), born out of a collaboration between the writer Curzio Malaparte (1898–1957) and the architect Adalberto Libera (1903–1963), two Fascists with talent. Casa Scalesciani is located at the top of a steep cliff, and has a serpentine plan. Much of the space inside is taken up by the steps connecting the rooms, which are on different levels: eight steps between living room and kitchen, five between kitchen and the single bedroom, three between the single bedroom and the double one. Two other bedrooms are (because of the irregular crest of rock) accessible only from the outside. It is a masterly work, described by the architect Jonathan Sergison as "seminal" in its expressionistic form, which derives from and portrays its improbable and eloquent position. Almost all its windows face into the Maestrale, the northwest wind that enters from the open sea, which lies about thirty meters lower down and can be reached by means of a flight of steps so steep it makes your knees tremble; a spring and swimming pool that seem to be carved out of the rock compensate for this psychological distance. The wall at the rear is almost blank. The roof is pitched, as in almost all of Ponis's houses. If Villa Malaparte is a perfect parallelepiped dropped into place from above, Casa Scalesciani is an imperfect and broken shape extruded from below—that is, from its foundation; it goes along with the undulations of the rock formation underneath, and through architectural articulations completes it, redesigning and reshaping it. Certain photographs capture its quasi-invisibility.

A third house-rock is Casa Bak, in the vicinity of Porto Rafael. Porto Rafael is the heart of Punta Sardegna, a promontory symmetrical with Capo d'Orso on the opposite side of Palau, below the monumental but almost invisible Savoy fortification of Monte Altura. Founded shortly before my parents arrived and gradually developed over the course of the following thirty years, Porto Rafael was born as an eccentric and alternative community, at once cosmopolitan and Italian, a small-scale but less opulent and snooty Porto Cervo. At its heart lies a picturesque square in the pueblo style, facing directly onto a small beach. The village, which has grown enormously over the years, now comprises hundreds of houses and villas of varying sizes that cover the whole of the side of the promontory looking toward Palau; here Ponis has built dozens of private houses.

In the volume *The Inhabited Pathway: The Built Work of Alberto Ponis in Sardinia*, the original conception of Casa Bak is described:

> The terrain offered two possible sites: one was a level, open clearing, ideal for building a comfortable house surrounded by a lawn; and the other was a steeply sloping site filled with enormous granite boulders, absolutely inadvisable for building on, since every aspect would be problematic. With great precision, masochistically and bravely, Ponis chose the latter. By doing so, he was able to leave the open area free and untouched, and over the years this has become the heart of the property around which the life of the inhabitants revolves. This is where they eat, cook, write, sunbathe, and play.

Note: the masochism regards the choice of the site on which to build, the precision of the intuition on which its design is based, the activities that determine the lifestyle of its inhabitants, and finally the importance that is assigned to the enormous masses of granite. Without these boulders, Casa Bak would make no sense. In his quest for the meaning of pleasure, Ponis made a sacrifice in its design: he preserved a place in the open where the proprietors could spend their vacation (without turning it into a garden), and located the functional program in two small house/rocks that contain the rooms in which to live and sleep. The architecture became a jigsaw puzzle, fruit of a geographical awareness in miniature that envisaged three phases in the elaboration of the design: a physical and mental survey of the area, a working plan drawn up largely in the process of construction, and a final survey at the end of the work. Casa Bak occupies the site by means that closely resemble the ones that have always been used by shepherds and peasants; something about it recalls Garibaldi's house on Caprera, which is, of course, a rural setting.

For over ten years, from 1966 to sometime around 1980, Ponis was a regular visitor to our house at Porto Ulisse during the summer months we spent there. It may have been precisely because he had designed a couple of hundred vacation homes by the sea that he never wanted one for himself. To me the reason for this seems obvious, since he certainly wasn't in Palau on holiday, but to live and work. On her way to Palau to do the shopping early each morning, Yasmin would drop by to see him in his studio, make a few phone calls (we still had no telephone), and then they would agree whether he was going to come to lunch, to dinner, or to both. Alberto, who almost always dressed in white, with long pants and a linen shirt, possessed the informal touch typical of certain English gentlemen, a sartorialism he may have inherited from Denys Lasdun and Ernö Goldfinger, two architects of standing with whom he worked in London in the early sixties. In his studio in Palau he wore a white single-breasted artisan's jacket, as people often did when pens and pencils were still used on drawing boards. When he came to visit, he would trot down the path, change in a room chosen at random, dive into the sea, and play water polo with us kids, teaching us some tricks while reminding us that he came from Nervi in Genoa, one of the elite centers of the sport. After a bit, my mother would shout to Rosa, our faithful housekeeper: "*Ohohoh, Rooosa, buuutta la paaastaa!*" And without fail my father would complain about the excessive volume, which he considered over the top. At the beginning of each season, around the middle of June, Alberto used to greet us with a terracotta pot filled with little plants of bright green basil, which were supposed to last us the whole summer. When we finished eating, we would play chess. In the afternoon he either went back to work in his studio or accompanied one of his *geometri* to check on his many building sites. One year he gave us a water polo goal that he had had made by a local carpenter, but it never stayed in place due to the movement of the waves and current. When he came to dinner, he arrived around sunset and stayed until late, long after we boys, exhausted after all the day's activities, had gone to bed.

He used to chat and joke for a long time with my mother in a mixture of Italian and English, by candlelight under the portico, with the geckos hunting insects on the walls and a green shot glass of sambuca in his hand.

—"But what is a cultured person like you doing here in Palau? An architect should be in the city, not in this desert! Moving the way you did straight from London to Palau was a step backward! Come and live with us in Milan!"

—"You're absolutely right, but as you know only too well life is made up of strange coincidences. I came here to Palau by chance for a few days and then I stayed. However, I find that the Sardinian landscape is a bit like the English one. At Porto Rafael there are several British people for whom I'm building a holiday house at the moment."

—"Oh, really? But rather than English it seems to me that the landscape here is Scottish, or South African. But how can you work in a landscape like this?"

—"This landscape doesn't distract me, it helps me concentrate. As an architect, I work with the landscape, and then, excuse me, but you are always drawing it too."

—"For me these rocks are almost works of abstract art. Henry Moore! Barbara Hepworth! It's strange, but we are each doing the other's work in a way. You would like to be a painter, and in this house I have acted as an architect! Don't you think so?"

—"For me these rocks are not abstract, but proper figures, like the houses I design. Look at the one over there, for instance, it's the skull of a goat, and the one just behind it has the beak of an owl."

—"Oh, come on Alberto, don't be silly ..."

With us kids and the guests who came and went, Alberto played a quasi-paternal role, perhaps because at the time he was not yet married and had not yet had two children of his own. In 1977 I decided I wanted to study architecture, and a few years later we had arguments about Aldo Rossi, whose architecture fascinated me as a student but he didn't like at all; he considered the complex of the Gallaratese in Milan a work of sadism. He was always a cheerful presence in the house, but never gratuitously facetious. Cultured and lively, he was also formal and respectful. He was the only person on the coast with whom my parents formed a deep and lasting friendship; all the others were seasonal and superficial. Between him and my mother there was an intense bond and a profound affinity. He got on with my father too, although he was less expansive and counterbalanced gaiety with reason. I am unable to imagine how he spent his long winters in Palau, for nine months every year from mid-September to mid-June. Although he worked on his commissions methodically and with concentration, he must have suffered from a degree of physical and cultural isolation. I can't imagine that his subscriptions to serious magazines like *The Architectural Review* from London, *L'architecture d'aujourd'hui* from Paris and *Casabella* and *Domus* from Milan were sufficient to make him feel part of a professional community. In the winter he would occasionally come to Milan to visit an exhibition or to see his friends. In the end this geographical isolation must have stimulated him to develop his own style, and an identity and characteristics all of his own. He used to make regular trips to the center of the island by car. He was asking himself if and how it would be possible to devise an architectural language respectful of both the identity of Sardinia and international tourism.

The mutual understanding with my mother stemmed from an agreement over the importance of the gaze, of imagination, and of experience, through the painting that presupposed a particular and precise analysis of things. Both had chosen to turn that stretch of coast into a self-portrait, and this was their bond. What Alberto really thought of the architecture of our house, so boxy and inorganic with its straight walls that had no physical or direct relationship with the rocks, so schematic and utilitarian, I do not know. I have spoken with him about it on several occasions, many years after his visits, but without ever obtaining a convincing response. Perhaps for him places and friends were two sides of the same coin. I think that he liked its isolation, the path, the three arches at the front, and the informal atmosphere that derived from the architecture. If my parents had already known him at the time they bought the land, it is likely they would have given him the job of designing it, although my mother was highly critical of his early houses, so sinuous and full of organic curves. If Alberto had been the architect of our house, he would probably have interacted with the rocks in a more empathetic way: articulating the form of the roof to a greater extent, connecting the bedrooms with the world outside and rendering the whole thing less static and more expressive.

At a certain point I had the idea of replacing the arches of the house with square openings, thinking that these would be closer to its spartan spirit and that they would let more light into the living room. I told Alberto, knowing that arches were not part of his vocabulary and thinking that he would agree with me. He grasped at once the sense of my idea, but rejected it: for him the arches were the heart and soul of life in the house, and as such were sacred and should be left as they were. We talked then of how my mother could have come up with the idea of the arches in the first place. Weighing his words carefully and with British phlegm, he told me that in his view the arches came from Tuscany, that is from Renaissance architecture.

The world of forms was always swirling at the root of my mother's painting. She signed her papers Yasmin, without adding either her maiden name Petersen or her married one Brandolini d'Adda. For many artists forms are reassuring and comforting, but for her there was a certain agitation and nihilism lurking within them. The historian of medieval art Carlo Bertelli, in his presentation of an exhibition of Yasmin's at the Teatro Sociale in Bergamo in 1997, wrote:

> 'Namib' means 'nothing', Yasmin once told me, and we have spoken at length of those lands where rocks, mountains, depressions, and the view of the coast and the sea are obliterated in a name that annihilates them all: Namib. Yasmin showed me the loose sheets of paper prepared with the rigor of a painter of the Quattrocento and hundreds of dogged studies, the results of hours of silence and research.

In the second half of the sixties, after a twenty-year break, Yasmin decided to return to painting and the tools of the trade, a moment that coincided with the beginning of the experience of the house at Capo d'Orso. The two events may have coincided but this was no coincidence. Everything around the house (the rocks, the plants, the sea, the sunsets) rekindled sensory perceptions in her that had sunk into lethargy; Sardinia was her Namib. In the same years, in her studio in Milan, she drew endless nudes, reacquiring the reflexes that in a painter link the hand to the eye. At the end of each day's work, she kept only "the good," tearing up and throwing away the rest. Models she had got to know at the Accademia di Brera sat for her, assuming the not very academic poses that interested her, positions and gestures observed and studied from personal experience and anything but orthodox points of view. It was when I was eight years old and used to go to her studio, located just a few meters away from the apartment in the center of Milan, that I started to appreciate the beauty, the curves, and the many different forms of the female body. The models weren't bothered by an amiable little boy wandering around and staring at them curiously; on the contrary they were amused. In the bureaus where I keep what I've inherited there are hundreds of these nudes, done in pencil, wax crayon, India ink, watercolor, silverpoint, perhaps even the odd tempera (but no oils), and just as many etchings, aquatints, dry-points, woodcuts, and linocuts (but no lithographs) that she had printed in the early years at the workshop run by Pietro Diana and Angela Colombo, and later on at Giorgio Upiglio's. Of the many highly distinctive collages she produced in those years, few remain in my possession. Trying to forget the fact that they were done by my mother, I find myself looking again at these works dispassionately, realizing just how powerful and generous they are, and how little they have to do with figuration. For her, nudes were pretexts for the composition of complex forms, of something that went beyond the human figure: bottoms, bellies, hands with their fingers, feet, thighs, knees, breasts, hips, shoulders, backs, chests, necks, and heads were absolute forms, each with a personality of its own. She was able to draw all the concave and convex curves that make up the female anatomy in an unbroken line, without even lifting the bamboo pen from the sheet of paper or the etching needle from the zinc plate. She used the brush itself to trace lines, produce chiaroscuros, prepare grounds, emphasize subjects, create glazes. The paper too was chosen scrupulously, its suitability established by touch. There are women lying down, standing, crouching, curled up, bent over, viewed in profile, from the back, from the front: almost always from vantage points that make it difficult to decipher their anatomy. Although she could throw off a rapid portrait, she was more interested in bodies than faces. The nudes, through their presence, anticipated the large installations in public spaces she created from the eighties onward, at the Palazzo dei Diamanti in Ferrara, the Casa del Mantegna in Mantua, the Casa di Giorgione in Castelfranco Veneto, and the Teatro Sociale in Bergamo. By dint of dogged repetition (as Bertelli so aptly put it), the nudes grew less and less recognizable and more allusive over time, metamorphosing into something else, and regressing—or progressing—to the state of primary anatomical forms: the rectangles of backs, the twin circles of buttocks, cylindrical torsos, the ovals of heads, the triangles of bent legs, the levers of wrists, the centerlines of backbones.

I like to imagine that on that day in 1964 when my parents discovered and fell hopelessly in love with Porto Ulisse, Yasmin already thought that the rocks were in reality anatomical parts. And I also like to imagine that, when she accurately and precisely produced hundreds of nudes in her studio in Milan over the winter, she was in reality abstracting and re-conceptualizing the rocks of Porto Ulisse. In parallel to her exploration of nudes, for years and with equal insistence she studied the rocks in front of and around the house, again through drawing; at a certain point, she must have confused figuration and abstraction, the real and the imaginary, what is physical and what is mental, Sardinia with her studio. Looking at and reproducing the Sardinian boulders, she must have thought that the abstract sculptures of Jean Arp, whom she revered, were figurative, and the figurative ones of Henry Moore, for whom she had equal admiration, were abstract. Many of her pieces are portraits of rocks, but those who have never seen the rocks at firsthand would mistake them for works of Concrete Art, derived in part from the material abstraction of the fifties

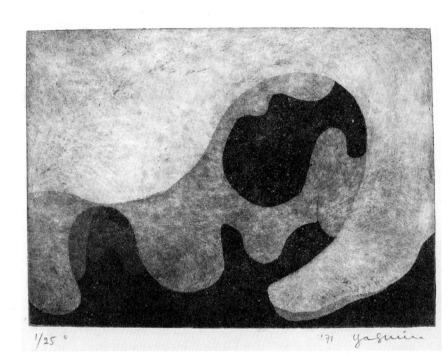

1/25 °   '71   yasmin

Yasmin Brandolini d'Adda, *Aquatint*, from "Rocce di Sardegna," 1971.
Archive Sebastiano Brandolini.

and sixties. Skeptical when it came to theory, Yasmin was happier talking of what she loved than of what she did. Through her drawings of the rocks, she wanted to show that there was no such thing as abstract art, since it was already present in nature.

While the forms of the nudes and the rocks lost their recognizability and got mixed up with one another, their presence and their aura survived, indelibly engraved in Yasmin's memory. The rocks in front of the house, both the ordinary and the extraordinary ones, occupied and troubled her, embedding themselves in her mind like fossils. Over the years they turned into silhouettes, hieroglyphs, halos, sheets of paper, gravestones, blots, installations, bones, compositions, words, musical notes, eggs, positive and negative impressions, all of them inescapably iconic.

One day, the two of us paddled our rickety little red fiberglass rowing boat *Caramella* under the belly of the Dinosaur, so that my mother could study its holes (whose profiles resembled nudes in a fetal position). I tried to keep the boat steady as she observed the patterns of the seabed and the light reflected by the water on the underside of the granite rock. Seated in the stern and tossed by the waves, she took out her pencils and made rapid sketches in her half-letter-format, spiral-bound album. These were the sketches that, once back in Milan, she would turn into the portfolio of aquatints *Rocce di Sardegna* of 1971. The drawings she made of sunsets (wax crayons and turpentine) would become something else: veils of hard-to-define hues, watercolors and gouaches with vague borders that to the unstable human eye appear to shift constantly, at once melancholic and poignant, the whole effect ethereal and technically difficult to achieve. Browns shade into purple, yellow turns blue without passing through green, green becomes red. The colors are laid on with a brush, sprayed or drawn. The white is often either pigment or paper, or both.

At the age of eighteen I developed a youthful enthusiasm for photography; I had been given an Olympus OM-1. Already conscious of their photogenic quality—and after visiting an exhibition of Edward Weston's work at the Hayward Gallery in London in 1977—I spent a summer photographing details of the rocks, and a few months later printed the best of them in black and white in the darkroom I had set up at Cison. The following Christmas I gave them to my mother. She was so pleased she had a box made to contain them. This box of prints became a family short-circuit: while my photographs emulated the drawings of my mother, her subsequent works—she claimed—were inspired by my photos. Today I'm no longer capable of figuring out the subject of my mother's drawings, nor of my amateur photographs, but this hardly matters. One of my pictures portrays the two holes, one oval and one round, located in the side of the Pyramid where we leave the house keys when we go down to the sea; their geometric perfection makes me wonder if nature used ellipsometry to make them, because the interior is as precise and smooth as the inside of an eggshell, or of a baroque ciborium. Sometime around the year 2000, Yasmin came up with the idea for an installation to be located between the arches of the cloister of a monastery in Verona; on each large sheet of paper—to be hung directly on the wall with four steel nails—she painted an egg. It would have been an abstract cycle of paintings but also decorative, deliberately repetitive. Each egg, of a different shape and color, was set against a background of a different color. Altogether, the eggs composed a repetitive classical frieze that conveyed a sense of spirituality and contemplation.

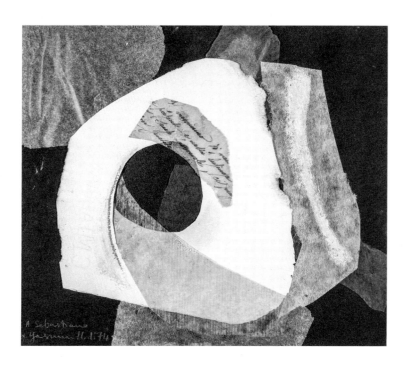

Yasmin Brandolini d'Adda, *Nude*, collage, 1974.
Archive Sebastiano Brandolini.

The portico is the empty space where everything happens. It changes constantly according to the time of the day, and everyone uses it as best they please. Without it, the house would lose its meaning. Here is a list, though incomplete, of things that have happened in it.

Lighting the candles. Checking that Palau and La Maddalena don't emit more light than they did the previous year. Falling asleep. Lying down on the granite bench. Listening if someone is coming down the path, and recognizing whoever it is from the steps. Setting up a small living room. Admiring the boats that head west in the morning and east in the evening. Sticking stamps on postcards. Putting the shopping bags down on the way in, or the garbage bags on the way out. Listening to the waves. Drinking water, or wine, or an aperitif, or a liqueur. Understanding how the shadows cast by the three arches work. Killing wasps. Working out how far away the *gozzi* fishing with lamps are. Asking what day of the week it is. Thinking about the market on Friday. Watching the sun go down. Checking if the towels are dry. Deciding who's going to sit on which side of the table. Painting toy soldiers. Drawing the rocks without lifting the pencil from the paper. Setting out the thirty-two chess pieces on the board. Wondering what time it is. Checking that the granite has not worn away over the years. Doing homework. Listening to the wind. Staring at a point in the sea and not letting our gaze be distracted by the waves, the current, or the reflections. Playing cards. Announcing that food is ready. Looking at the rocks in the moonlight. Having breakfast by ourselves. Chasing ants or moths. Cleaning the floor without using water. Reading a book. Treating a sea urchin or jellyfish sting. Reminiscing and talking about things to be done. Eating lunch and dinner. Writing down the shopping list. Proposing to prune the plants that obstruct the view. Scraping off the melted wax of the candles. Laughing out loud. Recognizing the constellations. Putting on sun cream or after-sun lotion. Calculating the proportions of the golden ratio. Discussing what it would mean to sell everything. Doing crosswords or puzzles. Identifying the fish and the crustaceans in the posters on the wall. Doing nothing. Taking photographs as a memento. Scrutinizing the clouds in the sky to predict the next day's weather. Doing floor exercises. Hearing the birds flapping their wings among the branches. Leafing through an old newspaper, thinking it's today's. Working out how many days are left before we leave. Playing a game of patience. Cutting fruit into little pieces. Telephoning relatives. Guessing the cost of the yacht designed by Philippe Starck that passes by us repeatedly. Redoing the hems of the cushions.

Of all the activities connected with the portico—which as a structure is a microcosm in itself—observing the boats, with or without binoculars, takes up the most time and gives the most satisfaction. Early in the morning the canoes pass by close to shore, the majority as solos but some in tandems, well-equipped and high-tech despite being a primitive means of transport as old as humankind. The canoeists like to pass very close to the rocks and often wave to us as if we were old friends, or even accomplices. Occasionally I invite them in for a coffee, and in this case they park their canoes in the swimming pool. I ask them where they're coming from and where they're heading, and tell them some more or less truthful anecdotes about my life. They tell me that if the weather is fine they do between twenty and thirty kilometers a day: "Last night we slept in Palau and this evening we'd like to reach some beach on the Costa Smeralda. Can you camp there?" In their words there is always some perplexity or doubt, whether it is about the weather, the effort, or the sea. They tell me I'm fortunate to have such a beautiful house in such a beautiful place, and go on their way encouraged and content. If they are not making a long trip in stages but just on a day's outing, I see them heading back to Palau in the afternoon. Around mid-morning, it is the turn of the rubber dinghies, rented from tourist ports along the coast (Palau, Cannigione, Baja Sardinia); they travel noisily and at high speed close to the shore, with the adults in the stern and the children in the bows, their legs dangling; when they catch a wave you can hear their screams of joy and you realize that for them it is a special day, an unrepeatable adventure which they will think back on with nostalgia over the course of the winter, wherever they may be. Observing all this is like watching a movie; we sit there without moving, and in front of us the world stirs and shakes, entertaining us whether we like it or not.

The sensation is even stronger when the sailboats go by, making no noise except when they change tack and then the sails beat against the wind, rolling like bass drums. Sometimes gigantic yachts pass by, with majestic masts and sails of dark gray Kevlar, phantom and somewhat disquieting vessels. We grab the binoculars and as true moralists observe them with morbid interest, trying to work out the size of the crew, how rich the owners are, the name of the boat, what flag flies at the stern, if it is the same one that went by a few days ago. Then there are the mega motor yachts, miniature floating cities almost as big as the ferries that run from Olbia to Genoa, Livorno and Civitavecchia. Their hubris includes a heliport, silent engines, a wake that produces waves which buffet the rocks and stir up the seabed. We ask ourselves questions without expecting answers: how many beds are hidden behind those stainless-steel portholes? For how many meters would all the couches upholstered in white leather stretch if you put them in a line? How many friends can the owners take with them on their gilded vacations? How can you breathe in the air of the sea when the air conditioning is on? Other craft we see include old but refurbished tugboats, nostalgic steamers resembling the *Patris II* on which the fourth CIAM (Congrès Internationaux d'Architecture Moderne) was held in 1933, acrobatic offshore powerboats hired from the hotels on the Costa Smeralda, and two-story vessels taking vacationers on a tour of the Maddalena Archipelago. Each motorboat makes its own noise, produces a distinctive wake, and follows its own schedule. The speed at which they are traveling can be calculated visually by noting the time it takes to traverse a stretch of sea between two fixed points of the landscape.

This incessant coming and going makes you ponder. In front of us pass sailboats and motor yachts owned by the super-rich of the planet, while behind us lie the semi-abandoned towns and villages of the Sardinian hinterland, beset by poverty and unemployment. Contrasting worlds brush up against and ignore each other, not speaking; the rich show no interest in the interior of the island, while the inhabitants of the interior think that tourism on the coast is a passing fad, one that sooner or later will burst like a soap bubble. The portico is the boundary—the *limes*—between these two worlds.

The portico is principally the house's dining room, its public space. More generally it is the place of conviviality where we stop and talk. It serves as a living room, because the living room inside is rarely used. Once upon a time lunch used to last a long time. It was elaborate and formal, and divided the day in two geometric halves. The *antipasti* were eaten on the rocks, and comprised *pane carasau* (Sardinia flatbread), pecorino, stewed octopus, marinated mussels, and white wine, served in fairytale fashion as we took a dip; half an hour later, hungry, we would sit down at table. The first course was pasta, usually spaghetti, with rich sauces (often made from cuttlefish) and in portions that today we would consider enormous; it was followed by fish, dishes made from what had been caught that day with the nets and the traps or had been bought in town, cooked in various ways depending on the species: fried, boiled, baked, sautéed, soused. For our part, we caught mostly bottom feeders, like mullet, seabream, conger, octopus, cuttlefish, on rare occasions a dory, a catshark, a sole or a dentex, even more rarely a lobster. There was no meat. And then there were the side dishes of vegetables, like *peperonata*, potatoes, zucchini, salad, cucumbers, tomatoes with basil. There was always a piece of pecorino, or a sliver of *peretta* (the Sardinian version of *caciotta*), or a spoonful of ricotta with a dribble of honey. Chopped peaches with sugar and a glass of *vernaccia* rounded things off, unless Rosa surprised everybody by taking out her ricotta cake with its crisp dark-brown crust, made from eggs, cinnamon, raisins, and pine nuts. At the very end of the meal out would come the tray of Sardinian pastries, dry on the outside and a sticky mixture inside, in Arab-inspired shapes, decorated with multicolored sugar beads.

Fishing was an important part of life, if only because to haul in the two hundred meters of net that was put out in the evening you had to get up early the next morning, by six at the latest. If it was windy, the nets stayed on the wooden jetty, and were not even put in the water. In good weather, we went out of the Piscina in the morning with the rubber Zodiac and *Caramella*. The two boats were brought alongside and tied together and we then headed into the dawn, following the reflection of the sun until the empty jerry can that we used as a floating marker was spotted and seized. We took turns pulling them up and if something special appeared everyone rejoiced. We returned around half past seven, when the sun was no longer reflected on the surface of the sea.

Once, on our way back, my father pulled the soft green packet of his Nazionali unfiltered cigarettes out of the pocket of his shorts, lit one with his damp wax matches, and I started to ply him with questions.

—"Papà, do you like better Palau or Cison?"

—"Well, they're such different places that it's impossible to compare them ... this is our holiday house, while Cison is the family home."

—"But for me this is a family home too!"

—"Of course it is! But it was built just a few years ago, and things change from year to year, and no one knows exactly how our lives are going to turn out. As long as we're enjoying it, it makes sense. The important thing is to look after it and use it."

—"But do you think there are people who wouldn't like this house?"

—"Good question! You know, a lot of them go on holiday to crowded places where they hang out with the same people they see all year in the city. But we like the summer to be different. I think that for some this house would be too adventurous. What about you though, do you think you'll still like it when you're grown up?"

—"I don't know, perhaps I'm already getting a bit bored with it. Every year here, always the same stuff. Also it depends whether friends are coming or not. It's a bit scary when it's empty. The other evening, when we heard those strange noises from the portico, I thought there was somebody on the path who'd come to spy on us. Do you think that's what it was?"

—"It's possible. Alberto said that the other night after dinner he saw a car with three people in it up at the parking place, and that it dashed off as soon as they saw him. He followed it but they were going too fast and gave him the slip. We need to keep an eye out, although I've noticed that because of the kidnappings there's a lot of police about."

—"Papà, do you think this is a luxury house that's worth a lot on money?"

—"This I don't know. In the end, perhaps it's not even very important."

Cleaning and untangling the mesh of the nets was a wearying and exacting task, largely because of the scorpionfish, the chameleonic little bottom feeder that we often caught, with a big head and full of venomous spines, but excellent in soups. Sorting the nets out would take until around nine o'clock, which is when the wasps would arrive, attracted by the strong smell. The mullet and the cuttlefish were easy to extract, while the crabs created terrible tangles and had to be pulled apart and then removed in pieces. We had three heart-shaped metal traps—they looked like Fausto Melotti's wire sculptures—for catching octopuses, some weighing two or three kilos, and the occasional conger; there was no need even to bait them with dry bread or cheese rind. When the sea was calm I dropped the traps from *Caramella*, but when it was rough I used to swim out to just past the Roccione in front of the house where they had their lairs at a depth of about eight meters. Still today, in exactly the same position, the tourist-fishermen arrive in the evening with their rubber dinghies, cylinders, and spear guns. Nowadays nets and traps are banned. I used to kill the octopuses, as chameleonic as the scorpionfish, by bending back their heads, and then I beat them energetically on the rocks by the water's edge, otherwise they would have been too tough to eat, especially their eight muscular tentacles, each with its double row of suckers. Our many attempts to fish from land or the boat with a line or rod invariably proved unsuccessful. Once we went trolling with someone who knew more about it than we did and there was a miraculous haul of mackerel, more than we were able to eat; my mother portrayed them in watercolor, with their silvery-blue livery.

The portico is also our party room, since in connecting up the different activities it acts as the hub of the domestic geography. Architecturally it signifies protection and shade. It casts a deep shadow that is hardly ever affected by the heat or touched by sunlight; the pillars and arches, thicker than the walls, produce their own microclimate. It is not an external structure added to the house, but a proper external room; some people call it a loggia even though it is not raised. In plan its proportions are 1:3, deduced from the fact that on the long side there are three arches and on the short side just one (of the same width). We could define these proportions as Palladian, or even Wittkowerian, although they can be found in every age and style. In section its proportions are 1:1; the ceiling slopes like the roof. Architectural details seem absent because they were conceived in terms of similarity and not of difference: a single step between the exterior stone paving and the portico, a single step between the portico and the interior; the same floor as the rest of the house and the same doors, windows and shutters; three square pillars, one of them on the corner; no wiring or plumbing apart from two electrical sockets and two hooks for hanging lamps or lanterns. The lateral arch contrasts the panorama in front with a sideways view of the scrub. The one concession to decoration is represented by two posters hanging on the only free wall. They are the sort you might see at the fishmonger's, one devoted to crustaceans and mollusks and another to the fish of the Mediterranean, with the names of the species in several languages along with their minimum and maximum sizes. Fifty years of Maestrale have consumed the original posters, but now there are new, almost identical ones.

Rosa Filigheddu, our housekeeper as well as factotum, accompanied us from the first to the last day of our holiday; in winter she came only to open up and air the house. She lived in the hamlet of Capo d'Orso with her husband Pietro, a cousin of the Filigheddu family who had sold my father the land. An ex-employee of the railroads, he had retired at the age of fifty and since then been idle, apart from going hunting. Rosa and Pietro had two daughters, Anna and Antonietta. The four of them slept and lived in a single large room of a small *stazzo*, immaculately clean and tidy and with an enviable double panorama looking toward Baja Sardinia and Porto Cervo in the east and Palau in the west. In *Il giorno del giudizio*, Salvatore Satta describes the home of some peasants in the centre of Nuoro, a sort of universal dwelling, similar to Rosa's: "Everything was brought to the house and everything was prepared there, and for this reason around the courtyard there was a series of outbuildings, each named after the particular gift of the soil stored in it: the oil house, the granary, the fruit store, and in addition there was the bakehouse, which was like an altar, or an Etruscan tomb. ..."

Rosa was not really Sardinian but from the island of La Maddalena, considered a world apart, an advanced outpost of civilization. She was plump, silent, short of stature and broad of beam, practically round, but nonetheless agile. She had ivory skin, for she had always scorned the sun. She really liked working for us, because she met people and found herself at the center of life. Her chubby hands were able to do everything with efficiency and precision: spreading the bedcovers without even the shadow of a crease, measuring the ingredients as she cooked with nothing but her eyes, pressing clothes with flatirons made of cast iron heated on the gas range without burning herself, making bedspreads and lace worthy of a museum, cleaning to perfection, and tidying up without leaving any trace of her passage. The work—apparently—cost her little effort, and both hurry and delay were alien to her;

every day she devoted three hours to cleaning, three hours to cooking and three to washing clothes. She seemed to be doing everything slowly, but it was not so. She could also read and write (far from common for her generation) and could solve the most difficult crosswords and puzzles. She got her first job in Genoa, where she had gone to stay with relatives, at the age of about twelve, dressing the dead at the morgue; her lips could often be seen moving as she said her rosary. In the early years, she used to come down from Capo d'Orso on foot, a couple of kilometers in descent on the way and the same in ascent to go home; later Pietro would bring her on his Lambretta; when Pietro died we used the car to pick her up in the morning and take her back in the evening; in her later years she didn't come at all, and then at the end of the morning we would take her the day's catch of fish in a basin; she would keep some for herself and give us the rest back in the evening, cooked to perfection. Sometime after she stopped coming she died. It was the end of a short era, because for us the house, Sardinia, and Rosa had always been one and the same thing.

The large table under the portico on which we eat has always been there, and was made by a joiner in Palau to a sketch by my mother. The top is a single piece of walnut, measuring 270 x 75 centimeters, although some claim it is actually rosewood. The legs are two white wooden crosses connected by a tie. It seats eight, including the people at the heads; and if we are fewer, it doesn't feel empty. Positioned carefully at the beginning of the season, it is not moved again until the house is cleaned and put into mothballs for the winter. It is a universal table, and as such is indispensable. Just as the house could not exist without the portico, the portico could not exist without this table. The thousands of hours spent around it, devoted to eating, playing games, reading, looking, and chatting, are the very life of this place. Once there was a second table of the same design but a bit shorter, that was used as an extension when there were more than eight of us, which between adults, kids, and friends happened often; at a certain point it was stolen, but by then there were fewer of us coming to the house and so it was not replaced. On the pink granite top under the posters of fish, one used to lay out the big and heavy serving dishes.

With the Maestrale, the wind blowing from the northwest, sailboats rounding the lighthouse on Capo d'Orso find the going heavy toward the lighthouse on Punta Sardegna and have to tack back and forth endless times; almost all of them go about in front of the portico, sometimes coming close enough to wave to us. The identical red boats of the Centro Velico Caprera (CVC), struggling not to sag to leeward, head toward the arches, taking advantage of the fact that here the seabed presents few surprises; it is a maneuver the instructors have repeated hundreds of times. For the learners the three arches stand as an icon, and the house as a mark.

One evening, three would-be sailors from the CVC are returning to base after a whole day out at sea: a Milanese accountant, a Neapolitan woman who owns a boutique, and a Roman architect. They speak freely without attaching much importance to what they say.

—"We always see this pink house with the arches and it has to be an illegal building."

—"No doubt. And it must be on public land as well."

—"Perhaps not, once you used to be able to build almost anywhere."

—"If it's like you say, then it wouldn't be so different from all the others."

—"Indeed … But on Capri for example there are many houses of this kind, and the legal and illegal ones are practically identical, there are no differences."

—"So how do you explain the fact that it's so isolated? It must belong to someone a bit strange, perhaps an artist."

—"Or a politician. There must be CCTV cameras around, otherwise there would be people on the rocks."

—"Would you stay in such an isolated place? Maybe they even rent it out …"

—"It's a beautiful spot, but I wouldn't sleep there. For me being on holiday means doing things with friends. I don't like feeling alone, but then I have never been really alone."

—"Let's not get too close to the rocks in front, there may be shoals and there's a strong current. Look, there's a man with white hair swimming among the waves. Let's go about where the others did. One, two, three ... about."

—"I'm almost sorry to leave the illegal house with the arches behind. It seems bigger from here. Look, near those strange rocks I think I can see another house, more camouflaged."

—"Perhaps it was a private allotment, certainly people with money. Crazy stuff, from a bygone era. As an architect, I've never had an opportunity of that kind. We ought to find out who it belongs to and who built it. Perhaps there's something online."

—"I'm worn out. Tonight I'd go for a double spritz, anything but water. But they're such bluenoses at the CVC."

—"It's going to take a while before we get back, five or six tacks. The wind is dropping but there are still waves."

I can only guess how my mother came up with the idea of the three arches. Perhaps they are a memory of the colonial porticos at Hermanus in the Cape Province where she went for her holidays as a young girl in South Africa, or of Brunelleschi's arches in Florence where she studied painting, or the two Palladian *barchesse* of Villa Emo at Fanzolo, the home of my parents' friends. But what I really think is that she conceived the arches without a nod to any kind of architecture far away in space and time.

Perhaps we need to use a bit of imagination, just as Yasmin did. The arch is a simple architectural form, whose significance is now settled, since its field of application has been reduced by reinforced concrete and steel. Arches bring the forms of architecture into direct contact with the solidity of engineering, and frame the landscape in a harmonious way. Both rational and sensual, they were well suited to the modus operandi adopted by my mother, who struggled all her life to resolve the contradiction that lurked within her, between being rigid and dogmatic on the one hand and creative and experimental on the other. I picture a scene. When she discovered this place with my father, my mother probably made a rapid sketch in her spiral-bound notebook of the two black holes—two eyes? two secret passages? two mouths? two musical instruments? two nostrils?—that she saw in the Roccione at water level in front of the house, making them indelible. She probably felt that the house should in some way resonate with these two holes. But how? In the end she came up with an analogical, not a literal, connection. Anyone looking out from the portico towards the sea can see the kinship between the two holes in the Roccione and the three arches in the wall because the resemblance is deliberate. Without the arches the holes would not be noticed, and without the holes the arches would no longer make sense.

Something else must have crossed Yasmin's mind while she drew the arches freehand, first in pen and ink in her sketchbook and then in grease pencil on the plywood template at a 1:1 scale. Something with a slightly bitter taste. She will have thought of all the arches—narrow, wide, pointed, skewed, irrational, oval, peeling, spectacular, precarious, mock, unfinished, irregular, vernacular, Provençal, Andalusian, caricatural, camouflaged—that infested the Costa Smeralda: for example in the first piazza of Porto Cervo, at the Hotel Cala di Volpe, in the phony villas of Vietti, Couelle, and Busiri Vici. To assert her own style, she wanted her arches to be clearly different: to be geometrical, pure and thick, perfect semicircles like those of the Renaissance, plastered and separated by square pillars, with no profiles or splays. And with no gaudy jasmine, bougainvillea, or bignonia to soften their intentional and schematic rationality.

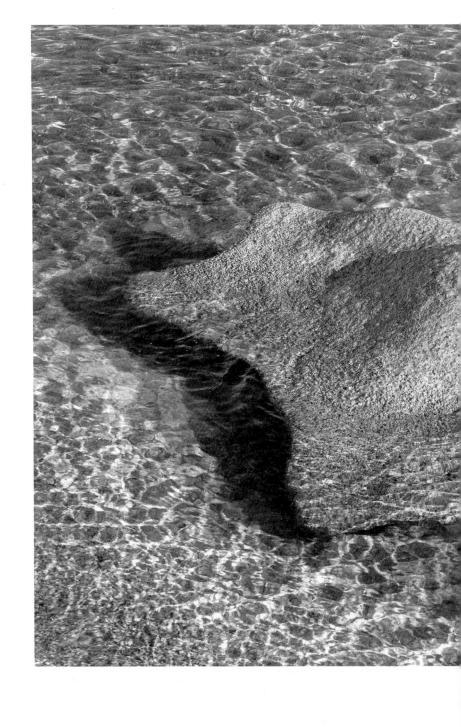

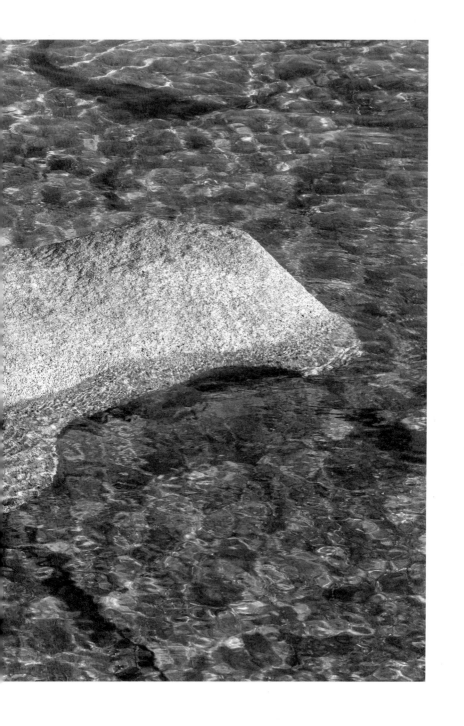

Gavino Ledda wrote in *Padre Padrone*:

Owing to the solitude, nature for me represented an undefined and intimate 'you': the only friend with whom it was possible to communicate without feelings of shame or unease. Every detail of the reality around me evoked a name that animated it and allowed it to speak to me. ... This intimate language between me and nature, which at bottom was the language of silence, had become natural and familiar to me almost as if reality were silence and things were its words.

Physical and mental solitude do not necessarily coincide. Solitude is often viewed in the negative sense of loneliness, linked to feelings of exclusion and isolation. But solitude can also have positive connotations, hidden virtues. It could be a case of that hermetic *nunc stans*, that eternal present of which Thomas Mann speaks in *The Magic Mountain*, a book he asks us to read twice. While it is not hard to imagine that physical isolation can be planned, it is more difficult to plan the solitude of the mind. Can there be a house whose identity is rooted not only in its isolation, but also in solitude? Is there an architectural language or character capable of stimulating the atmosphere or the spirit of solitude? Does solitude have to be an absence, or can it also be understood as presence? Is it a contradiction to think of the "presence of solitude?" I first asked myself these questions thirty years ago, when I went to Sardinia with my father for two or three days at the beginning of December; he fled by air after just one day, and I stayed behind with the car and the ferry ticket. I dined alone in the cold and afterward reluctantly set about translating a convoluted text by the architect Vittorio Gregotti from Italian to English, seated at the desk on the mezzanine, in front of the nautical chart of the Maddalena Archipelago, if for no other reason than to make myself sleepy. The air was damp and with several electric heaters turned up to the maximum, drops of condensation formed on the terracotta floor, in direct contact with the ground. There was no sign of life other than my own: no boats on the sea, not a breath of wind, no lapping of the waves, no creaking of doors or windows, no household appliances running, no animal or bird in the vicinity. I remember it as an experience at once poetic and eerie. There was only the clacking of the keys, the type bars, and the platen of the Olivetti typewriter as it moved to the next line. If I stopped and held my breath, I could hear the beating of my heart and the gushing of the blood through its ventricles, two sounds I had never perceived distinctly before; distinguishing and hearing them was for me a demonstration of the all-encompassing silence and isolation of the house, there all alone on that out-of-the-way stretch of coast. It occurred to me then that all this had been architecturally and consciously intended, and could certainly not have been a matter of chance.

Where physical isolation is concerned, the rocks and boulders form the equivalent of a ring of walls; the house can be seen from the sea but it is a feat to land; there is no garden to act as a buffer for the wilderness; there are no lights outside; the dirt road is a dead end; the other three houses that complete the parceling out of the land are perceptually distant; to reach the car you have to walk up a path that further separates the house from the rest of the world; the yellowish glow produced by Palau at night is three kilometers away, the lights of Porto Rafael and La Maddalena six; no one lives on the islands of Santo Stefano, Spargi, and Caprera and at night they are dark. There is not even room for a domestic worker to keep you company; there is no television or satellite dish, at most a radio with faltering reception. From here the inhabited world seems far away and hard to reach. A curious phenomenon of perception comes into play: the house appears dangerous viewed from the outside world and the world outside seems threatening viewed from the house. We are trapped in a cage, de facto castaways. Physical isolation turns into mental solitude and gets under your skin, resulting in a metamorphosis of the sensations that make up your personality.

At a certain point, during the construction of the house, my father considered the possibility of parceling out the land to allow the building of ten or so small houses above and around the parking place, with their own direct and separate access to the sea. I know this from a still legible blueprint I found in a folder; but in the end he did nothing. Some have argued that my brother and I would be rich today if our father had been bolder. I suppose there were two reasons why my father abandoned the idea; at the age of thirty-five he must have known he didn't have the stuff it takes to be a real estate developer, and in fact there was nothing brazen about him and he would not tell half-truths even if he stood to gain by them. In addition, being by nature careful and prudent, he must have realized that a development of the land behind us, however inconspicuous and well handled (today we would say environmentally sustainable), would have altered the equilibria of the place, civilizing it and turning it into something banal: more traffic, more people, more noise, more hassles to deal with and problems to worry about. In short, the Brandolini family would have lost that vein of inspiration that makes Sardinia something quite unique for us.

Here, the radical isolation predisposes you to contemplation. At various moments of the day (and not necessarily sunset) the conditions are right and you fall (or are raised) into a state of unconsciousness and unreality; this state is produced in part by natural phenomena, like the succession of light and shade and the rhythmic cadences of creation, but it is also induced by the architecture, bare and devoid in expressiveness or empathy. Its disarming nudity generates a feeling of solitude; it is a sense of solitude similar to the one conveyed by a solitaire, a tree isolated in the middle of a field or a meadow. The house reduces to a minimum, indeed avoids any mediation or conversation with the nature and scenery around, apart from what derives from the fact of being in that precise location and not anywhere else. Its geometric and square plan has nothing in common with the anthropomorphism of the rocks and the junipers, but clashes with them; it has simply been set down in the place where it stands guard and is at the service of a stretch of coast.

There is an affinity of form between the red houses (many abandoned, others upgraded) built along the country's roads by the ANAS (Azienda Nazionale Autonoma delle Strade), the state company responsible for the construction and maintenance of Italian infrastructure, and the farmhouses of the Po Valley that Aldo Rossi describes in his *Autobiografia scientifica* (many now vanished, only a few surviving). The feeling of solitude also results from the fact that the house, devoid of details, makes no attempt at perfection in its measurements and shows no interest in philosophy. The 1:100 scale drawings offer little information, with their straight and perpendicular lines and 90-degree angles. There are no joints between materials, because the aspiration was to adopt only one material, an objective that was successfully achieved. No iconography, no authoriality, no expressiveness, no coloring, nothing too comfortable, nothing to suggest refinement or aesthetic pretensions. The overall effect of all these absences is a detachment that provides the setting for a certain sense of mental solitude. All this reminds me of my family's self-control, but it is also a trait of the proud character of the Sardinian people.

Geographic and architectural solitude have three effects on us: an awareness of the passage of time (i.e., the unnecessariness of clocks), a profound experience of the weather (i.e., the variation of the sky and the light), and a desire for immobility (not to be confused with laziness).

166

There's no point in looking at the clock, you just need to know how to read the shadows. In front of the house, which faces due north, the sky is wide open. In the morning the sun rises in the east over the crest of the island of Caprera (the exact position shifts each day of the year), climbs and reaches the zenith behind us, and then descends and disappears behind the crest of Punta Sardegna; the sun follows a course that runs parallel to the profile of the mountain behind, a clean and flawless arc, as clear as the one that it would describe on the dome of a planetarium, as precise as the three arches of the portico. On June 21, the summer solstice, it rises almost in the northeast and sets almost in the northwest; you can follow it with your eyes the whole day. On March 21 and September 21, the days of the two equinoxes, it rises and sets exactly in the east and the west, where the two extensions of the line of the facade meet the horizon. On December 21, the winter solstice, the sun stays hidden behind the mountain all day and the house remains in perpetual shadow. The north front is almost always in the shade, and this is providential as it keeps the portico cool. Only from March 21 to September 21, in the morning and evening, does a bit of direct sunlight touch the portico and enter it edgewise, illuminating the insides of the arches and the floor and lapping against the wall of the living room; this is why these two moments of the day, the times of breakfast and the aperitif, are special. Northern Europeans find it hard to grasp that at this latitude—41°10′45″12 N—shade is something of value, ignorant of the fact that even shadow has its luminosity, a fact of which the painters of the Renaissance were well aware. In Sardinia many of the houses built for tourists face south, and in the summer are exposed to too much sun and too little wind, with the result that they are uninhabitable. Palau is in good company, located at the same latitude as Naples, Istanbul, New York, and Beijing.

It is not just from the shadows, but also from the shades of gray on the rocks that you learn to tell the time of day. Early in the morning the shadows of our bodies are as long and fragile as the sculptures of Alberto Giacometti, and the granite takes on warm and languid beige tones, by way of the film of moisture that the night deposits on its surface. Later the granite dries and turns almost white, and the contrast between the parts lit by the sun and the fissures in shadow is almost dazzling. Toward the evening it turns a pastel shade of red; at this point the eroticism of the rocks is evident and can no longer be ignored. We feel as if we are surrounded by breasts, horns, buttocks, teeth, lips, vaginas, thighs, penises, navels, and biceps, by "apophises and phalanges" as my father orthopedically described them in a poem in his first slim volume *Da un monte rovesciato*, published by Vanni Scheiwiller in 1973. The place is a clock and the house is a sundial; together they make up an instrument for the measurement of the passing of time, both exterior and inner time. On the rare gray days when the light does not change, the instrument seems to have jammed.

"Observe the stars," Pythagoras is said to have answered when he was asked what was the sense of man's presence in the world. The Pole Star—scientific name *Polaris*—remains motionless on the perpendicular above Guardia Vecchia, the highest point of La Maddalena, and to see it all you have to do is look straight in front at night, where it hangs 40° above the horizon. Its constellation, Ursa Minor or the Little Dipper, rotates like the hand of a clock and makes a complete turn of 360° every 24 hours; it is a nocturnal timepiece, for use when the granite doesn't cast shadows. At night, in July and August, after dinner and before going to bed, the two constellations of Ursa Minor, and Boötes can be seen just to the west of the Pole Star, the former with the star Alioth and the latter with Arcturus; to the north the cross of Cygnus is visible and to the east, over Caprera, the W-shape of Cassiopea and the alignment of stars of Andromeda, where if there is no moon and you know where to look it is possible to make out the galaxy of the same name, two and a half million lightyears away. Around three in the morning, for those who suffer from insomnia, rise the constellations of Auriga, Perseus, and Orion, this last typical of winter nights, spanning the northern and southern hemispheres. Putting our trust in natural clocks produces mixed sensations. On the one hand we feel strong and in full possession of our physical and mental faculties, courageous and self-sufficient; doing without things like a watch or a cellphone makes us feel we have superpowers. On the other, having to rely on many but always vague small signals from nature in order to tell the time of day makes us feel in constant danger, lost and with nothing to hold on to, really breathless. Everyone reacts to this state of confusion in a different way. Some guests, put out by the fact they had not realized it was already after one o'clock, prefer not to eat at all that day. Others, unable to resist the daily urban habit of a coffee and the newspaper at the bar, go to Palau every morning. Watching variations in the shadows, colors, waves, wind, and stars in order to tell the time of day or night is hypnotic. We enter a potent psychophysical dimension, a state of intense physical and mental perception that acts on our personality and behavior. The day of our arrival, we feel alert, hyperactive, and doped up, having lost our points of reference and needing to adjust to another reality. The day of our departure the reverse occurs, as we ask our bodies to reset and readjust to what we could call the usual pace of our life. The first day lasts an eternity, the last the blink of an eye. The perception of the length of the other days is subjective, but rarely right.

I was struck by an expression I came across in a book: *meteorological ethics*. For me, meteorological ethics signifies not having to look for information on the weather beyond what is provided by our senses. Here at Capo d'Orso meteorology is founded on sensations that have become knowledge. In his treatise *Meteorology* Aristotle speaks of the air and the water of the earth, of earthquakes and fire, and of what had already been written by his predecessors. He also discusses clouds and their height, the sea, winds, thunder and lightning, auroras and rainbows. He dwells too on marine erosion, suggesting that the coast is something that cannot be considered always either sea or land, since "all this changes in course of time." Here the weather influences our style of life and our behavior: it is on the basis of the wind and the temperature that we choose whether to go down to the sea, if and where to stay at home, whether to go into town, what to read, what games to play, whether to eat or drink, what to drink or eat, whether to swim or walk, to sleep or stay awake. Here, right here, as well as a meteorological ethics, there is a meteorological mode of behavior. The eyes and the ears will be open to the currents and the colors, the breaths and gusts of wind; if the wind drops we slow down, if it stops we stop too. If we really needed to make forecasts of the weather, we could devote ourselves to observing the flight of crows and listening to their calls, an ancient branch of divination called *coracomancy*.

The desire for immobility is also induced by the solitude of the architecture. The fact of not feeling any need to go elsewhere is not easy to explain; perhaps it is comparable to certain practices of gymnastics that require slow and calm movements derived from yoga or qigong. We are happy to stop here because this is a dead end that contains and offers stimuli, distractions, wonders, variety, and questions to unravel. As if we were prisoners in a *Wunderkammer* filled with drawers whose contents are unknown, or browsing through the index of an encyclopedia crammed with cross-references, or lost in a building with an infinite number of corridors and rooms, here we feel the need to slow down, breathe slowly in and out and distill our senses. By letting everything that is outside us and the place we occupy (the sea, the air, the birds, the clouds, the boats) move, we benefit from the fact of not moving.

On the masonry shelves of the house there are still some books written by Anglophone authors in the colonial or postcolonial mold, read in their time by my parents. Freya Stark (1893–1993), Evelyn Waugh (1903–1966), Laurens van der Post (1906–1996), Alan Moorehead (1910–1983), Lawrence Durrell (1912–1990), Patrick Leigh Fermor (1915–2011), Vidiadhar Surajprasad Naipaul (1932–2018), and Bruce Chatwin (1940–1989) were all restless travelers, always wanting to be somewhere else with a pen between their fingers, vagabonds who anticipated the cheap globalization of the last thirty years. Theirs are books which show that just two generations ago human beings still felt themselves to be explorers, nomads, and migrants. In parallel, this house for my mother and father was the result of an existential flight.

Since Roman times Sardinia, as an island, has been used mostly as a place of confinement and exploitation. From the house we can see the islands that make up the Maddalena Archipelago, whose function in recent centuries has been largely military. In the distance (like a decided brushstroke in one of J. M. W. Turner's watercolors) runs the gray ridge of a mountain range that is another island, Corsica. A few tens of meters in front of us in the sea, masses of granite emerge from the water, and they too are islands—islands for swimming to. Too small to be put on a map, they worry people in boats because they are treacherous and dangerous. They belong to the marine world rather than that of dry land. The fact that they seem to float makes them look light and graceful, but in reality their robust foundations lie on the bottom of the sea, at a depth of around ten meters. Though small, they are solid. Cormorants, seagulls, and terns rest there, dry out, chatter, and cover their surface in droppings, an activity in which they are sometimes joined by crows and herons. Being public land, they belong to everyone and no one. When the children were still small and innocent, as a reward for their first ventures into the water, I told them they were mine, but when they were bigger I would give them one, so they would be able to put up a tent and spend the night on it. They believed me and got so excited that they stopped complaining about the effort involved in learning to swim.

On the desk on the mezzanine, halfway between the ground floor and the first floor, there is a nautical chart in black and white of the Maddalena Archipelago. You can study it for hours, looking at the shape of the islands and the sea, which cover roughly the same area. Like all maps it explains and confuses, and is difficult to relate to the reality of what you see. This archipelago is peculiar in its extent, in the proximity of the sixty or so islands and islets that make it up and in the narrowness of the arms of the sea that separate them (in comparison, for example, to the Aeolians, the Tremiti, or the Hegades). There is a sheltered stretch of sea facing Sardinia and open sea beyond Caprera and La Maddalena. Some islands are mountains, others are flat. Forts and lighthouses mark out triangulations that let you imagine naval battles. Among its more alluring traits: the coast filled with projections and indentations in reddish tones in the south of Caprera, the round and compact shape of Spargi, the fact that Giuseppe Garibaldi tried to establish a viable farming activity on Caprera, the lagoon on which converge Santa Maria, Razzoli, and Budelli (it was here, on the celebrated "Pink Beach," that Michelangelo Antonioni shot one of the scenes of his disquieting movie *Il Deserto Rosso* in 1964). The map of the archipelago enchants the adolescents, who redraw it in silence, with particular precision and empathy.

The waves of the sea batter the swimming islands all year round, massaging and smoothing them. We are allowed to stroke their sensual surfaces without being considered indiscreet. They serve as destinations that can be reached with a few strokes, as if they were both physical and spiritual marks. Here swimming should be seen as movement, as a means of locomotion and not a sport. Over the years the islands have become idols that observe us and encourage us as we approach, let themselves be touched, advise us when it is the right moment to leave and finally bid us farewell. Leeward and windward they are not the same. And they are also the pickets of a border that defines the area in which we can swim.

The island in front of the house is the mother of all these island-rocks, and does not have a proper name, apart from Roccione with a capital R. In the winter, I redraw it by memory, as it is for me a fixed presence, an obsession, a scar left on my gaze. The Roccione is also frequented by the kids when they want to go diving or isolate themselves and sulk. It is separated from dry land by a channel five meters wide in which there is a strong current, especially when the Maestrale blows; it is also possible to wade across the channel, with the water coming up to your bellybutton. Beyond it is the open sea. About fifty meters long and roughly oval when viewed from above, it is in reality composed of ten or so separate granite boulders of varying size, stuck together in such a way as to create the illusion of just one mass; in the fissures, which you have to be careful not to fall into, you can hear the air and water squabbling over the small amount of space available and producing spurts, belches, farts, gargles, and eddies. Each of us is free to see whatever we wish in these cavities, shapes, and round holes. I, for instance, see the head of a horse just like—although it is made of granite and not marble—one of the horse's heads carved by Phidias that are in the British Museum; I feel upset when others fail to recognize what is unequivocally the head of a horse by Phidias. Then there are the two dark holes that look like eyes and which inspired my mother to design the three arches of the portico. It is easy to feel misunderstood and betrayed in front of these rocks; language reveals its limits and is found wanting before these manifestations of nature. I will not expand on the other things I see embedded in the Roccione, things like a diving board, a keel, a buttock, a fish, an open book. In the slight undulations of its smooth back, pools of sea water, when they dry out, yield good salt which can be useful in emergencies.

Swimming anticlockwise around the Roccione with a strong Maestrale is like fighting against a mountain torrent. You dive in after throwing the towel in a cleft on the leeward side that seems to have been made for this purpose. The first stretch is relaxing, with the current in your favor and no more than a few ripples in the channel that separates it from the mainland, barely deep enough; to avoid getting scratched, it's better to keep your strokes just beneath the surface of the water, like the paddles of a canoe. After rounding the eastern end, you make a sharp turn to the left and increase the strength and rhythm of the movements of your hands and feet; the sea is choppy and throws up spray, and suddenly grows rough and deep; there are always some fine fish darting around beneath us. Next comes the most difficult stretch, the one against the current where we mustn't look back like Orpheus did in Hades, because here the wind and current buffets us mercilessly and if we relax for an instant we're swept back ten meters; urchins, limpets, and anemones cling to the sloping surface of the underwater rocks. We reach the western end, where two rock formations, a round one and one that looks like a beak, are both good for diving; below, at a depth of four meters, there are dark and undulating meadows of Neptune grass. At this point the waves whipped up by the Maestrale are coming from behind us and we can stop swimming and let ourselves be carried along on our backs to the place from where we dived in three or four minutes earlier.

A hundred meters west of the house, two islands, always previously referred to as the islets, have recently been renamed Castor and Pollux, the two stars in Gemini. Their height is derisory, forty odd centimeters above mean tide level, but important, because they may disappear over the coming decades. Once you have emerged from the water and climbed onto one of them, you have the thrill of feeling like a castaway, just as they are often depicted in cartoons in the summer papers. All it takes is a little wave to make them disappear, only to resurface like the back of a whale. Their existential fascination obliges us to become aware of our body and the small amount of space it takes up. Each islet, with an area of ten square meters or less, is surrounded by deep water. The narrow channel that separates them has a bed that is part sand, part rock, and part mud. Lying here you are overcome by a feeling of bliss, but you can't stay for more than a few minutes.

Another big rock, also called roccione but with a little r, is located to the east, in the direction of Caprera, where the sun rises. There and back is a distance of around five hundred meters, a quarter of an hour; it's a swim that demands some physical effort, because under normal conditions, with the Maestrale blowing, the current is in your favor on the way there but against you on the way back. It requires just the right amount of effort to roll back any sense of guilt generated by the laziness that tends to go with being on holiday. It's a contemplative swim, given that the scenery you pass by is lunar and unreal. You are caught up by the current of the sea, and the noise of the splashes that your arms make when they meet the waves keeps you company, as if someone were whispering in your ear. As you swim you have to use your eyes to establish your position and make sure you're on the right course. There are many points of reference that help us get our bearings, underwater and on the surface: the dead weight of a hundred kilos or so that was once attached by a chain to a buoy which could be used to moor a small boat; the fault of basalt that runs all the way across Sardinia and dives into the sea right here; a shoal sought after by colonies of urchins; the Santo Stefano lighthouse, an abandoned tire that has been lying on the bottom for years without ever disintegrating; a couple of gas cylinders; some pottery shards that are signs of a shipwreck (from how long ago?); an overhanging rock of friable granite; a few fan shells (*Pinna nobilis* is the name Linnaeus gave them) that have reappeared after years in which they were nowhere to be found. Altogether, these signals draw a map filled with triangulations that interact with the landscape and tame the sea, turning it into the house's garden. Next to the roccione, there is a little beach of coarse sand that attracts canoeists and where it is easy to find traces of fires and moments of happiness.

If we go past the roccione, we come to its alter ego, the roccino or little rock, a mere pimple. It is located where the coast bends to form a gulf, on the opposite side of which stands the white lighthouse of Capo d'Orso. Despite its small size and proximity to the shore, it is visible from a distance and looks bigger than it is. It intercepts all the waves of all the winds that blow through here, and throws up a lot of spray; it's a kilometer from Caprera and by definition the destination of our long swim. At almost a kilometer from the house, the roccino is a coveted goal; you have to pace yourself and paradoxically it's better to go slowly, allowing the combined rhythm of your strokes and your breathing to become automatic, almost lulling you into sleep. Anyone who doesn't want to undertake such a demanding swim can split it in two. The first day you can walk to the roccino along the coast, hide your shoes and other personal items under a bush, and swim back; the next day you can do it the other way round.

Once we were waiting for a friend to return from the Costa Smeralda with a *gozzo*, and as he was late we began to worry because the Maestrale was against him and blowing strongly. Watching for the *gozzo* to appear on the horizon, we found ourselves continually catching sight of the roccino, which confused us; at moments it seemed as if the roccino were the *gozzo*, although our suspicions were aroused by the fact that it didn't appear to move. In the end the *gozzo* did turn up and was plainly moving; our friend returned safe and sound, if a little shaken.

The Roccione, Castor and Pollux, the roccione, and the roccino are all barely visible when you're swimming, because they are out of focus and almost level with the water's surface; our vision, blurred by the salt, the waves produced by the wind and the motorboats, the spray and the turning of the head to breathe means that our sense of direction is almost intuitive. To reach the swimming islands, we try to stay in visual contact with the seabed, mostly covered with seaweed in greenish tones, so as not to lose our way. When we can no longer see the bottom and become hypnotized by the rays of sunlight that penetrate the blue sea, tracing a boundless visual pyramid, it means that we've gone off course and are going to have to raise our heads and carry out a triangulation. A few strokes toward the coast, and we're back where we should have been, inshore. The swimming islands are sculptures that contain grottos, balconies, fissures, chutes, and sheer drops. Working out how they would look if the sea were to recede takes a bit of imagination. Out of the water the granite forms create turbulence, and in the water currents; air and water have much in common. If when swimming with goggles or a mask you are lucky enough to spot an octopus, a cuttlefish, or a mullet, it is such a fleeting glimpse that observation is almost impossible; it is like an apparition. I've always preferred sea urchins, anemones, starfish, and mollusks, with their shells clinging to something, to fish, as they move slowly and with circumspection.

Although swimming and walking have much in common, at one time we didn't walk. In Sardinia walking and running were regarded as absurdities. At Capo d'Orso you went swimming and sailing and played tennis; it was only natural, in that this was the logic of a holiday. Then at a certain point something must have changed, but I don't remember exactly what and when. Perhaps a scooter broke down and someone ended up going to Palau on foot, a journey of about fifty minutes, and enjoyed it. Or perhaps there was a guest who made a habit of running on the dirt roads, and we caught the bug. Or perhaps, after the establishment of the National Park and the consequent ban on fishing, we no longer possessed a rubber dinghy or a sailboat and, no longer knowing what to do in the late afternoon, had to invent other pastimes. At this moment, along with the style and times of our holiday, our perception of the landscape changed too, and so walking assumed a new significance. For us today, the word Sardinia conveys the ideas of both swimming and walking, inseparable from one another. Both share the rhythm of breathing, the absence of haste, the fact that the effort involved is distributed in space and time, and the precision that derives from repetitive movement. They present physical well-being as something quite different from exertion and competition.

There are three roads connecting Palau with Arzachena, but only one of them is worth walking along. It's dangerous to do so on the Orientale Sarda, the interminable road linking Cagliari with Santa Teresa, 370 kilometers of bends from which you can hardly ever see the sea. It is unpleasant to walk on the coastal road that passes through Cannigione, which has been straightened, widened, and equipped with traffic roundabouts and parking lots: a disjointed and unpredictable linear city now runs along its edges. But you can walk on a third road, which traverses the countryside through numerous ups and downs, passing by old *stazzi* and a few new *agriturismi*, along which the scrub has silently reclaimed the abandoned *tanche*, as sheepfolds are called in Sardinian. For years it was unsurfaced, but it has now been asphalted; it has tight bends, humps, bramble bushes filled with blackberries, ruinous stone walls with crooked old wooden gates, and new gates in a flamboyant style, with mailboxes and intercoms. Its new inhabitants have planted olive trees instead of cork oaks, Mexican cactuses instead of prickly pears, pink oleanders instead of yellow broom. In the pastoral Sardinia described by Deledda and Dessì, up until sixty years ago there were paths and sheep tracks everywhere the flocks wandered; today, now that the shepherds and their paths have vanished, only roads are left. Arzachena, the destination of our fifteen-kilometer-long walk, is a charmless town whose center is composed of the amalgamation of a number of *stazzi*; it has a ring road, a few supermarkets, a fishmonger's, some nuraghes, and a giant's tomb; the sea is only a few kilometers away but feels distant since it cannot be seen. According to Bandinu, Arzachena is little more than the service center of the Costa Smeralda, much of which lies within the territory of the municipality. To get there on foot takes three hours; then someone will come to pick you up and take you home by car.

The usual destination for a walk from the house is Palau, four kilometers away. With backpacks empty on the way there and full on the way back, you go there to buy enough to last two or three days; for bottles of water and wine it's better to organize things differently. Many people, of various ages and degrees of fitness, make the Capo d'Orso-Palau trip in both directions; in the summer you see processions of walkers and runners; the Ponente in your face slows you down and dehydrates you, but in the opposite direction it makes you fly. The procession resembles a propitiatory rite. Capo d'Orso is also the hamlet from which you climb, at dawn or sunset, up to the Orso, or to the fortress named after it. From the top there is a panoramic view of the archipelago, with the channels dividing the islands, the lighthouses and granite and scrub contending for the best positions. The sea insinuates itself everywhere, with shades of blue that change with the depth and the currents, and yachts lurking like hawks in the most coveted roadsteads. One understands now why the archipelago has historically been the most favored military position in the Western Mediterranean, presiding as it does over the only passage between the Tyrrhenian Sea in the east and the Sea of Sardinia in the west.

The fortress is abandoned, a place from the modern era that could be mistaken for an archeological site; few tourists defy the signs and dare to climb over its rusting gates. While its abandoned state may stir feelings of melancholy, it could also be seen as a method of conservation. It reminds one of Dino Buzzati's description of Fort Bastiani in *Il Deserto dei Tartari* (1940), whose central theme is—as the author declares—the "flight from time," the same reason why today many people go to Sardinia for their holidays. Buzzati said that:

> [T]he idea of the novel came out of the monotonous nightshift I was working at *Il Corriere della Sera* in those days. It often occurred to me that that routine would never end and so would eat up my whole life quite pointlessly. It's a common enough feeling, I think, for most people, especially when you find yourself slotted into the time-tabled existence of a big town. Transposing that experience into a fantastical military world was an almost instinctive decision.

The fort is not a surreal movie set, but a tangible reality: the ruin of a building in which to walk, get lost, hide, and perceive the passing of time. The weather and thieving antiquarians have already carried off the best pieces of wood and iron; but the granite, of little commercial value even when skillfully modeled and sculpted, is almost all still there, as it is too heavy to be taken away. A road runs downhill from the fort (almost invisible) to the lighthouse (highly visible), creating a curious architectural dichotomy. It is the same lighthouse that we have already seen from the roccino.

The Fortezza di Capo d'Orso bears witness to a century and a half of uninterrupted wars, and preparations for war, in Europe. In 1793 the kingdom of Savoy defended the archipelago against an attempt at invasion on the part of Napoleon Bonaparte, until Horatio Nelson inflicted a definitive defeat on the French in 1805. In 1851, after the First Italian War of Independence, the House of Savoy strengthened the defensive structures of the area, only to abandon them shortly afterward. In 1887 the fort was enlarged with a view to controlling the Strait of Bonifacio and defending Palau. Although Sardinia was not directly involved in the First World War, the fortresses of the archipelago were strengthened and camouflaged anyway. The Fortezza di Capo d'Orso was supposed to defend the military harbor on La Maddalena during the Second World War, but was unable to prevent the sinking of the cruiser *Trieste* by Allied bombers, on April 3, 1943. In 1950 the wreck was salvaged and sold to the Spanish, who wanted to turn it into an aircraft carrier, but the plan came to nothing.

The lighthouse can also be reached by foot from the house along the coast; for some this is a walk, for others a climb. You have to repeatedly use your hands or leap like goats, and at a couple of points you risk ending up with wet feet. Instead of a real path, there is an abundant repertoire of alpine passes in miniature, including chimneys, crevices, smooth rock faces, and dihedrals. Your knees and ankles have to work hard, and you need to wear sneakers. In the space of a few meters, the granite passes from being sound to being rotten. If you slip or stumble, though, you're not going to hurt yourself. The branches of the junipers don't get in the way, because when they grow so close to the sea the wind flattens them and they creep along the ground, as do the rosemary bushes. When we walk this way we go past the roccione and the roccino; but swimming is faster. This small expedition, which we try to make every year, reminds us that this stretch of coast is still wild, far away from everything. For this invigorating sensation we are grateful to the Filigheddu family, who after selling my father the lot on which he built his house, decided not to sell any more land. If they had, there would be hundreds of little villas with gardens here today.

Palau is our local town. It's not as rural as San Pantaleo, born out of the aggregation of a number of stazzi in the hinterland of the Costa Smeralda and now given an elegant makeover. It is not disciplined like La Maddalena, where the urban layout of the center is the orthogonal one of a military garrison. It is not topographically spectacular like Santa Teresa, which forms a twin town with Bonifacio on the opposite coast of Corsica, like the ones that stand on both banks of a river or on either side of a mountain ridge, like Nuoro with its two opposing centers of San Pietro and Sèuna. Nor is it a service center like Arzachena. Palau is none of these things, and has never shown any ambition to become other than what it is. Its main efforts seem to have been devoted to not taking a turn for the worse; maintaining a bit of decorum, it solves its own problems, usually belatedly (that is, when they are already well embedded), hoping in this way to avoid making mistakes. It is our village of reference where we go not so much because we want to but because we need something, be it food, medicine, the newspaper, or to treat the kids to an ice cream cone or guests to a glass of vermentino. "Mais non!" Maigret would exclaim at this point, always ready to expound the opposite point of view to what has just been said. Palau is something else too: the place where we encounter other specimens of the human race, and where we establish a relationship with the rest of the world, when we tire of the poetic isolation of Porto Ulisse. If Palau were not there, we would want a place exactly the same, although perhaps with a few more quality food stores. For us going there is a minor expedition, like going for a long walk in the mountains, a mix of exertion and pleasure: we have to remember to bring the wallet with the kitty, draw up a shopping list, find some sturdy bags, and agree on who is going to do what and at what point we are going to meet up for coffee. The four kilometers that separate Porto Ulisse from Palau are a trifle, but one that psychologically entails a mental leap. You don't go to Palau just to do something practical, but also to stoke an emotional desire, the urgent inner need to go home, in order to experience a special joy descending the path and seeing the rocks when you return. The roofs of Palau are visible from the house across a stretch of sea and a strip of land called Punta Nera, at a distance that is the right distance. It is the same distance that separates Villa Madama in Rome from Piazza del Popolo, the countryside from the city: less than an hour on foot.

The Palau of the sixties, when my parents landed there with the *gozzo*, was different but not better. At the time the local inhabitants were almost all dressed in dark clothes and did not expose any part of their body to the sun except their faces and hands; only young men who worked in the open would strip down to their undershirts. It was—I always thought—a matriarchal society. The women worked hard running the house and family, while the men grew old, sitting for years on stone benches next to their front doors, nattering and complaining about the world as they waited for evening to fall, at which point they would go off to play cards in one of the bars down at the port. There were two restaurants. On the walls were posters with the grim faces of wanted bandits, offering a reward in millions of lire, an indecipherable number with many zeros. Children slunk from one side of the street to the other; the stray dogs belonged to everyone and no one and were mongrels, hungry and thirsty, but never aggressive. Only the main street, Via Nazionale, was asphalted but without gutters. The other roads, unsurfaced, just threw up dust. The sidewalks were not clearly marked, while traffic circles, the two bypasses on the inland side and along the shore, one-way streets, and road signs simply did not exist. There were many stores where you could buy food and few selling clothes; today it's the other way round. A couple of stores sold fishing gear. The artisans, such as the carpenter, blacksmith, and plumber, had stores facing the street. There were no offices, apart from the post office. Almost all the buildings were small urban *stazzi*, only one-story high; in one of them, with a small garden at the back, lived Alberto Ponis with his cats. The few two-story buildings looked like small *palazzi*, with their entrances and symmetrically arranged balconies and cornices. There was no trace of modern or contemporary architecture; indeed no one had any idea what modernity was, except the four-story, three-star hotel where vacationers went to sleep and a public housing block that looked as if it had been copied from a post-Bauhaus architecture manual. Tourists could be recognized from a distance and were black swans, anthropologically different from the locals. They had uniform tans, wore colored clothing, straw hats, T-shirts and shorts, with sandals and espadrilles on their feet. They did not understand the Gallurese dialect and laughed and talked loudly. They shaved with care, their hair was neatly cut, they went to the pharmacy for aesthetic reasons and not just for medicine, frequented the only travel agency, went to Mass only on Sunday, bought little bread, paid with checks, and owned recent models of car. We of the Brandolini family belonged to this category.

Today, unlike then, you are regularly faced with the problem of finding a place to park, although in reality the spaces are just well-hidden and in the end you always find one. Palau's uniformed meter maids, however proud and strict, cannot cope with the volume of traffic in July and August, which creates Gordian knots around some of the crucial commercial ventures, such as the ice-cream parlor, pharmacy, tobacconist/bar/newsdealer, bakery,

Palau in the 1950s—postcard.
Archive Sebastiano Brandolini.

fishmonger, and tiny Sardinian *pastificio*, which also serves as a delicatessen. The time devoted to the frantic search for a parking place (unless you decide to leave the car in the multistory parking garage) gives the passengers an opportunity to make good-natured comments on the vulgar attire of people in the street, on how muggy the air is, or on which stores have closed and what has taken their place. Local gossip.

There are three things in Palau that I would be sorry to see disappear one day; but I put my trust in the treacly nature of bureaucracy and the inertia of the status quo. I would be unhappy if the relationship of Palau with its landscape were to change again. Palau is half headland and half gulf, or rather both things at once. It has always pointed its finger at La Maddalena, and from its tip run the ferries that shuttle back and forth between the two ports, on weekdays and holidays, by day and by night, independently of the calendar (except on days when the strong Maestrale and the currents reduce the maneuverability and safety of the ships). From the house the ferries are model boats whose appearance punctuates the day (some have inscriptions on them in Swedish, a sign they used to be in service in Northern Europe); they sound their horns when private yachts pass too close to them, trying to reestablish the hierarchy of the seas. But Palau today is also a gulf; the postcards show us that on the stretch of coast leading to Capo d'Orso eighty years ago the kids went swimming in the nude, and at night people fished with spears and lights. Palau has expanded in this direction in order to become modern in its own way. It was here in the thirties that it enlarged its Gothic-style cemetery (to which a church was later added); in the fifties it built its low-cost apartment block in a rationalist style; in the sixties a hotel with a facade of arches in the style of Ischia; and in the nineties developed—timidly at first and then with more determination—a district of condominiums and small villas bristling with balconies, so densely packed that they almost rub up against each other. The gaps were then filled with the town hall, emergency medical service, and shipping office. In reality, from 1970 to 1990, Palau grew in all directions, wherever it was possible: toward Capo d'Orso, toward the beach of the Rada di Mezzo Schifo, around the harbor, along the link road to the Strada Orientale Sarda, and onto the slopes of the mountain behind. Similar in this to all the other villages on the Sardinian coast, Palau is certainly no exception. Its resident population increased from 1,800 in 1960 to 3,800 in 2010, doubling at the expense of the villages inland, whose population over the same period fell by 30 percent on average. It has remained compact and dense, inventing for itself a type of terraced condominium, containing hundreds of apartments with balconies facing onto the sea.

I would also be sorry if Palau were to lose what remains of its narrow-gauge railroad line, which has a preindustrial air. The railroad station at the port, a stone viaduct that cuts the old quarter in two, the bed of the tracks, and an unused level crossing are all still there. The tortuous line, constructed around 1930, led to Tempio Pausania (Palau's municipality until 1959) and continued to Sassari, the administrative center of the province and the second-largest city on the island, one hundred and fifty kilometers away (Sardinia is in no way lacking in history, as many people still believe). In recent years an attempt has been made to turn the line into a tourist attraction with a "green train" running on in summer, but the idea seems to have been abandoned.

I would be sorry too if the weekly market, held every Friday in the parking lot in front of the marina, one day moved or vanished. It is a market lavish with products and in the summer fills up with stalls that tempt tourists with souvenirs, such as knives from Pattada, coral from Alghero (but the women say that it is from China), or Sardinian carpets made who knows where. The stall that used to sell baskets woven from asphodel has disappeared as if by magic. The ones devoted to fruit and vegetables are brimming with fresh produce, but then strong arms are needed to carry the twenty kilos of products needed for the coming week. For their attractive appearance and pleasant odor, we buy the seasoned cheeses with waxed rinds for which Sardinia is famous all over the world; the pale ricottas (made from cow, sheep, or goat milk) will be savored with a teaspoon of honey (made from asphodel, thistle, sainfoin); and *bottarga*, or fish roe, which we can't do without as it puts everyone in a good mood and is precious. We get our wine, mirto, beer, and water from a little store that has a good range and has to be reliable as it serves the yachts moored in the harbor. We don't eat much meat but for this there is a butcher's specializing in skews to be grilled on the barbecue, something we don't use at the house because of the risk of fires. When it opened in the industrial area, the supermarket was thought to have brought a wave of progress and convenience, but in the end it hasn't proved much use; we go there only to buy pasta, kitchen towels and toilet paper, detersives, and garbage bags.

The current parking lot and marina sum up the history of urban planning in the center of Palau. The site of the parking lot was once occupied by the dirt soccer field, while in the place of the marina there were little rocks in shallow water where we used to moor our Zodiac. On the soccer field, around 1970, a wonderful, unique game was played: Palau versus the Rest of the World. The outstanding members of the Rest of the World team were the players on holiday at Porto Rafael or on the Costa Smeralda, celebrities of the caliber of Franz Beckenbauer, Gerd Müller, Roberto Boninsegna, and Franco Cordova. That year Gigi Riva's Cagliari had won the Italian championship, turning everyone into supporters of Sardinian soccer; among the spectators was Manlio Scopigno, Cagliari's "philosopher" coach. The Palau team, hairy, robust, and enthusiastic, enjoyed itself, went in hard and had little to lose; the players shouted incomprehensible messages to each other in the local language. The international stars had fun too, but with only Adidas sneakers on their feet feared for their ankles and kept jumping with both feet together to avoid direct contact. Goals were scored with mutual satisfaction and in Solomonic fashion the result was a draw, but what really counted in the end were the handshakes and fraternal cross-cultural embraces. Shortly afterward the old soccer field was turned into a parking lot, still with a surface of beaten earth, and the little rocks became a concrete wharf with bollards and a sad line of palm trees. The soccer pitch was moved a long way away alongside the panoramic road, to a place only accessible by car, and was covered with green turf thanks to the use of sprinklers; no one goes there any longer. In this way the town lost a public place of amusement, ritual, and companionship overlooking the sea.

To make up for this loss, Palau laid out its first tourist piazza. Triangular in shape and set out over several levels on the Via Nazionale, it was designed by Ponis, and it is not his best work. The piazza, which has a small theater-auditorium, is ennobled with an abstract sculpture by Giancarlo Sangregorio, a friend of my parents. Nonetheless, the feeling is that Palau still lacks a true public square capable of accommodating the town's current 4,500 winter residents and 35,000 summer vacationers (in contrast to the open spaces seemingly created at random as a result of building projects carried out over the years). Tourist villages often think they have no need for public spaces for their own inhabitants; this is evident at Porto Cervo too, where the public spaces are intended exclusively for the tourists. Many of Palau's public spaces are decorated with granite boulders removed from the landscape that had patiently modeled them over the millennia; realizing that these rocks lose their fascination and significance once moved, the town recently decided to use trees instead, but these are more like symbolic totem poles, given that they offer little shade. Old and knotty olive trees have been transplanted onto the roof of the multistory parking garage, where they don't look at all happy.

On summer evenings and nights, Via Nazionale gets pedestrianized and becomes Palau's main public space; the diligent traffic policewomen block the only access for vehicles, and the road turns into a *corso*. Suddenly fashionable and nocturnal (at one time everybody was in bed at this hour), Palau fills up with lights, stalls, fritters, knickknacks, and little booths. Multicolored ice-creams are snapped up and placed in the hands of excited children, who run about and trip over one another. The section of the parking lot in the port that hosts the weekly market is turned into a fair, visited by people of different ages from all over the coast, summer vagabonds who sleep in the houses, in the apartments, in the hotels, on the campsites, in the villages, and aboard the boats. The line that once sharply separated participants from visitors at the local festivals, a line of which the anthropologists and sociologists of Sardinia have written, has grown so thin it has almost vanished. It is hard to distinguish the Sardinians from the Continentals, the Italians from the foreigners, the vendors from the customers, the rich from the poor, and the itinerant peddlers from the residents.

That Palau offers this confusion and social mixing is to its credit. The town has never specialized; it has remained simple and a bit banal, without pretensions but inclusive. It has its harbor and its bars, restaurants, and shops, which include a hardware store, a stationer and a repair shop; pedestrians and cars somehow coexist; there are a post office, a gas station, a cemetery, and a large church. These are presences that in today's liquid world we can no longer take for granted, for they have vanished or are absent from many other towns and villages.

F

or years it seemed that there was no political, social, economic, urbanistic, anthropological, or cultural thread running through the many projects carried out in the northeast of Sardinia from the sixties to the eighties, the years of the economic boom. Each project seemed to go its own way, with no evident logic. Then all of a sudden a guiding thread, a connection did appear. All the projects, depending on the criteria adopted, were either villages or resorts; modular, flexible, and repeatable, some resembling rabbit warrens. The module has been repeated a multitude of times, with slightly different forms. Until 1960, there were only four villages on the stretch of coast that runs from Olbia to Santa Teresa (Golfo Aranci, Cannigione, Palau, and La Maddalena); today there are twenty or so.

The new ones were all born as seasonal resorts offering a sense of well-being derived from the presence of the sea. Pleasure is a right, thought Sigmund Freud, and a primary and inalienable good of humanity. Porto Rotondo, Portisco, Cala di Volpe, Porto Cervo, Poltu Quatu, Stazzu Pulcheddu, the hotel on Santo Stefano, Porto Massimo on La Maddalena, the Centro Velico and the abandoned Club Med on Caprera, Porto Rafael, Costa Serena, the Isuledda, Porto Pozzo, and La Marmorata are all resorts. Looking beyond their form, identity, and the social class on which their success is based, each satisfies and gives its own contemporary twist to the transhumance that is so deeply rooted in human beings—and from which comes our idea of adventure. Today it is customary to work and earn money in a metropolis for ten months of the year and then take off for a village for the remaining two months of freedom. If on the one hand the metropolis and the village are alternatives, together they form a successful alliance that betrays a certain ambiguity; as the metropolis grows and ramifies, it increasingly comes to resemble a mega-village, made up of a multitude of micro-villages. Among the peculiarities of the seasonal metropolis of tourism that winds like a serpent to the north and south of Olbia is the fact that it has almost no true residents. For ten months of the year it returns to its primordial demographic state. In the boom years of Sardinian tourism, the universities and architecture magazines devoted little attention to the emerging new Italian geography represented by the seasonal villages. Academic circles still regard them today—be it Porto Cervo or Porto Massimo—as vulgarities of no cultural value, lamenting their impact on the region and the landscape and making specific accusations about their consequences: property speculation, the expansion of infrastructure, land take, the betrayal of local identity, the violence done to nature, the lack of beauty. Many recent resorts are not even marked on the maps. While this attitude is comprehensible given the mediocrity of many of the projects, such alarmism has precluded the possibility of making the sort of distinctions that would have been necessary in order to create conditions favorable to a generalized and intelligent quality. What do the neo-resorts of Sardinian tourism have in common, apart from being located on the edge of a sea of great beauty, one of the finest in the world? And what differentiates them?

These neo-resorts all have a public space, normally a piazza or *piazzetta* facing onto a small harbor with boats; the initial objective of the developer has always been to create a community of tourists that would identify with a physical location. The expression *community of tourists* may seem a contradiction in terms, but this was not the case some fifty years ago, when flights cost much more and someone who bought a house by the sea did so with the idea of putting down roots and making it last, both as an investment and as a place for the family. The *piazzetta* of the village of Porto Rafael, for example, has not changed since its completion over half a century ago. Constructed to look as if it were already old and conceived as a *hôtel de ville*, it is a mixture of the architecture of Capri and Andalusia. Rafael Neville—its eccentric founder—was an impoverished Andalusian count, the histrionic son of a film director, who claimed to have had a vision of the place which he had to follow. In front of a modest beach sheltered from the Maestrale, he realized his dream in 1961, anticipating the Aga Khan; his resort is a frivolous and playful, scenic and crooked place, consistent with his belief in Shakespeare's adage that all the world's a stage, as is also demonstrated by the family coat of arms that he affixed next to his private balcony facing onto the *piazzetta*, on which he was wont to appear naked on his birthday, like a true Adonis. Porto Massimo, Poltu Quatu, and Porto Rotondo all have their little squares on the water. Porto Cervo, which plays the part of the capital of pleasure on the coast even though it's not even a municipality, has many piazzas on many different levels and of many different sizes; in the end it is a village-square that is founded on the unchecked proliferation of public space given over to *flâneurs* devoted to aperitifs and shopping. San Pantaleo on the other hand originated as a true rural village, perched on the rocky mountain that dominates the peninsula of the Costa Smeralda and laid out around a central courtyard with a small church that was used for collective agricultural purposes; the yard gradually lost its practical function and became a civic square; today San Pantaleo has been gentrified and boasts villas surrounded by lawns studded with centuries-old olive trees (imported along with the grass), open-air dining with tablecloths, scented candles, and little else.

In the early years of the boom, the neo-resorts preferred condominiums to private houses; this preference for a certain urban atmosphere and collective nature can be discerned both on the Costa Smeralda and in the area of Palau, and can be traced back to the density of all the urban centers in Sardinia, where the houses are piled one on top of the other without any apparent order or hierarchy. After a few years the real-estate market started to require a greater diversification of building types, and since then single-family houses and small villas have proliferated, their selling price dependent on the distance from the sea and the value of the materials from which they are made—and certainly not on the quality of their architectural design. In the sixties and seventies, a lot of new tourist ports, named Porto Massimo, Rotondo, Quatu ("quiet"), Cervo, or Rafael, encouraged a homogeneous social frequentation, made up of vacationers who met up there every summer, conducting themselves not just as proprietors but also as architects and custodians of the very idea of Sardinia.

The scale, originality, and ambitions of the new villages that were created in Sardinia between the sixties and seventies went hand-in-hand with an awareness of the original unspoiled nature of its coastal scenery, and this consciousness had an influence on the architectural identity of the villages themselves. There are some who argue that the preservation of the environment and the interests of property developers are not necessarily incompatible, as long as they are handled adroitly. Others, such as Italia Nostra, have never believed in the possibility of a synergy between business and nature. Established in 1955, in response to the often deleterious effects that rapid economic, social, and demographic changes of those years were having on Italian cities, towns, villages, monuments, regions, and landscapes, the association is dedicated to the protection of the country's cultural, artistic, natural, and environmental heritage. Twenty years later, one of its founders, Giulia Maria Crespi, also set up the Fondo Ambiente Italiano, based on the model of the British National Trust. She never fell for the ambiguous idea of environmental protection implemented by the Consorzio Costa Smeralda and, on a smaller scale, the Consorzio Porto Rafael. In 1958, in a display of foresight, radicalism, and determination, she acquired a large plot of land (one hundred hectares, featuring various *stazzi*) a few kilometers to the west of Porto Rafael, with access to the beach and dunes of

Porto Rafael—postcard.
Archive Sebastiano Brandolini.

the Cala di Trana opposite the island of Spargi. However physically close and philosophically remote they may be, the speculation of Porto Rafael and the conservation of the Cala di Trana provide food for thought. Giulia Maria Crespi, coming from an exceptionally wealthy family, built nothing new on her land and let the landscape take its backward course in time, returning from a pastoral state to that of wild scrub.

Even the most determined detractors of the planning and papier-mâché architectural style of the Costa Smeralda often find themselves having to admit that some of its neo-tourist resorts have been set gracefully in the landscape. Especially during the initial phases, the sites occupied by the resorts were chosen with prudence. It was all part of an advertising campaign aimed at creating expectations, needs, and demand for a colossal and complex property development scheme. Sites were chosen for their access from land and sea. With no topographical reliefs or geological outcrops, they were located on sandy shores where the sea was calm, not very deep, and sufficiently turquoise. Over time swimming pools, wharves, and piers could be added to expand in many directions. It had to be possible to turn the *natura naturans* of the dry and yellow Sardinian landscape into something semitropical and luxuriant, fresh, and green all year round. Over the following years, ever stricter regulations and environmental restrictions prevented the northeast of Sardinia from being completely covered with unscrupulous developments. Today, the Costa Smeralda is half a wild place, as Giulia Maria Crespi (who died in 2020) romantically wished it to be, and half a gigantic development scheme, as has always been its consortium's commercial aim.

Porto Cervo is the grand capital village that epitomizes these splendors and flaws, the magnet, both alluring and irritating. Its mock-antique style was planned with meticulous care. From the moment of its first programmatic and architectural conception, it embodied the tourism of pleasure and lust. Intentionally, in order not to promote bad thoughts, no cemetery was built. From the outset its founders had had in mind the winning combination of house and boat, and were not interested in distinguishing between the two. Here we find, even in the view of many Sardinians, the true Sardinia; sixty years after its invention, the planning departments of many municipalities consider the architecture of the Costa Smeralda to be genuine and honest, and insist that it be used as a reference for new projects. The visionary Porto Cervo is based on a sense of wonder and dream, and sets out, like a good drug, to obliterate the banal reality of our everyday existence during the rest of the year. It has been successful and brought prosperity and visibility to a place that was previously considered of no value. Before it came to be known as the Costa Smeralda, this stretch of land was called Monti di Mola (also the title of a song by the Genoese singer/songwriter Fabrizio De André, who was kidnapped in Sardinia in 1979 and released months later). While the Sardinian anthropologist Bachisio Bandinu has fiercely criticized the effrontery of Porto Cervo and its extraneousness with respect to everything around it, the Swiss historian Nele Dechmann speaks with detachment of its planning and architecture, without a hint of criticism. In the booming Western Europe of the fifties and sixties many new tourist villages and grand hotels were built, not only on the coasts of the Mediterranean but also in the Alps and the Pyrenees, on the shores of lakes and the Atlantic.

This is how Prince Karim Aga Khan, the leading original investor in the Costa Smeralda, recalls his first visit to the place:

I had got involved in the scheme somewhat sight unseen, and then I went to Sardinia. To get from Olbia to our property took about eight hours. I realized I had made a very poor investment: I would never be able to enjoy the beauty of those places. It was like building a vacation home in the Amazonian forest. There was nothing there: no water, no electricity, no roads. If we wanted to go to that part of Sardinia for our vacations we were going to have to build everything ourselves. So I went ahead and turned the venture into a proper investment.

Words that make clear the immense distance that lay, at the beginning of the sixties, between the physical reality of Sardinia and the mental expectations of anyone arriving from outside. So what was

Hotel Cala di Volpe—postcard.
Archive Sebastiano Brandolini.

it in reality, the Costa Smeralda? Bandinu explains it to us in his book *Costa Smeralda* published in 1980, to which I am indebted:

> Eighty families scattered over a hundred or so *stazzi* in an area of five thousand hectares. The soil was good enough for subsistence farming; the sea was an extraneous element, there was no trade ... Extreme isolation: no roads, three hours by horse from the nearest town, which was Arzachena. ... The elements on which the production of the *stazzo* was based were: ten goats, two cows, three pigs, ten hens. The economy of annual provisions: cheese, grain, pork products, all in small quantities. The land was not subject to exchange, there was no division of labor. People went to Arzachena for salt, shotgun cartridges, the occasional handmade iron tool, and medicine.

Since Gallurese culture had no knowledge of the economic forms of commercial capitalism and tourism, there was no common language or shared understanding of rights between the investors and the peasants. Two different codes, one pre-agricultural and one capitalist-touristic, came into collision and it was almost inevitable that suspicions, misunderstandings, and short-circuits would arise. And so it was that the real-estate and architectural mythology of Porto Cervo was forged. The locals had inalienable plots of land on which a price had never been placed, and regarded the billionaires as benefactors. If for the tourists with yachts the Costa Smeralda was a promised land, for the peasants their arrival was a miracle. Bandinu relates a tragicomic anecdote, one that raises a smile. A peasant, wondering what this land was good for, came up with his own answer: "For us nothing! Let the multimillionaires have their fun here! Lucky them! They're certainly not things for us ..."

From the outset, the Consorzio Costa Smeralda was determined to respect the environment while turning it into an attraction. The first building code laid down precise rules in this regard, and the development plans determined the positioning and growth of the brand; stratagems were invented to ensure that property development and preservation of the environment were reconciled, in the end creating situations that today, with hindsight, we might define as suburban. Initially, the village of Porto Cervo consisted solely of a wharf for the boats, a beach, a square ringed with a few hotels, stores, apartments, a parking lot, and some villas in the environs; the architectural model was the same as the one previously adopted at Porto Rafael, although on a different scale and with different ambitions. Nothing was to look new and everything had to be done in just the right way to make it appear mythological, cloaked in an aura of fable, almost as if it were a ruin. Capable architects like Couelle, Busiri Vici, Mileto, Sasaki Associates, Mossa, and Vietti were agreed on the fact that Porto Cervo should be a simulacrum, and one whose retro taste unequivocally signaled the vacation. Their clients were happy to go along, not batting an eye at the shift from facades of steel and glass to ones of peeling plaster. In *Il giorno del giudizio* Satta argues that Sardinia is a land that needs idols, and that here the idols were linked with self-destruction and solitude:

> ... the enraptured town of Nuoro had a need for idols (like all other towns in Sardinia). ... This sort of idolatry was not in contradiction, as it might appear to be, with the destructive spirit that set the Nuorese against one another. ... This same hope led them to create phantoms ... but the real hopeless cases were the idols that imagination or hallucination had brought into being, so that they sought salvation in an artificial solitude.

In the sixties and seventies, while Porto Cervo entrenched itself, eroding the coast and turning it into a *limes* stretching for several kilometers, semiotics permeated the whole of Italian society, from politics to the arts, and including the landscape and architecture; Porto Cervo belongs to this precise moment in history. Its shoddy empiricism comprised bent walls, girders covered with twisted tree trunks, roofs with no geometry, flights of steps built for solely aesthetic purposes, curves of variable radiuses, sloppy coats of plaster, deliberate dysfunctionality, a profligate expenditure of energy dressed up as poverty and deluxe materials. Here, tourism was a ball, and architecture danced. Bandinu argues that everything here can be traced back to the political economy of desire, including the sea, water, sand, beach, rocks, and bushes, and in the end asks himself: "Is it a process of disguise and disclosure or is it a technique of control?"

I meet a friend who has been working for years in the hotel real-estate sector. He likes neither tourism nor being a tourist, and as a result feels isolated. When he travels, mostly for work, he conducts himself as much like a local as he is able. I ask him some questions.

—"What is tourism?"

—"Tourism is physical distance from where you live. The farther you go, the better the vacation. No one goes on vacation in their backyard, like my grandparents used to."

—"Whether we like it or not, are we all tourists today?"

—"I think so. It's not easy to distinguish tourists from locals. In this nice bar where we've come to drink a bottle of wine, we're all mixed up, people from Milan and from elsewhere, residents, holidaymakers from far away and from close by. United by the fact that we're all tourists. Without tourism, many activities in many places would have to close down; it would be a real social trauma. This bar is full, but the one just fifty meters down the road, where there's not the same atmosphere, is empty."

—"Are you happy it's like that?"

—"I am not supposed to be a moralist. It's the reality of the world we live in. In my view, mass tourism also acts as political cement, contributing to peace in the world. It's a phenomenon of consumption as well as of identity, which may seem a contradiction but is not at all."

—"Why not?"

—"Because experience and authenticity are what people are looking for when they go away from their homes. At home many people live sad lives that negate the very concept of experience, but on vacation they rally and are transformed, independently of their age, income, sexual preferences, of where they go. Whether it is Sardinia, the Red Sea, or Thailand no longer interests most people. The hotels, the B&Bs, the resorts, the Riviera Romagnola, the Costa Smeralda, they are all pure entertainment today, theatrical sets of the unexpected, at a reasonable price of course."

—"Why do people go on vacation?"

—"People go on vacation because they need something to fill their free time. The mass vacation exists because the trade unions fought for it, which is something we often forget. And I think it is still the case."

Today, it is not easy to distinguish here between what is a port and what is a hotel, or between a resort and a village. We give the same thing different names depending on our mood and who we are. On the island of Santo Stefano, opposite my house, there is a place that in the summer is all four of these things at once. It used to be called Villaggio Valtur ("Valorizzazione Turistica"), before a tour operator went bust in 2018. The island of Santo Stefano is triangular in shape, has an area of about three square kilometers, and at its highest point reaches one hundred meters; but to our eyes it looks square, as well as bigger and higher; grasping distances and scale in this landscape devoid of references can be complicated, as we already know. Santo Stefano has three monuments devoted to the passage of time: Neolithic remains have been found (as on Spargi and Budelli); there is an unfinished thirteen-meter-high granite sculpture of the Fascist hierarch Costanzo Ciano who was supposed to have been buried here in a cubic mausoleum with a granite lighthouse at its rear (the work was suspended in 1943); and there are the remnants of a NATO base that was operative from 1972 to 2008 and at which four Los Angeles-class nuclear submarines were stationed. The Villaggio Valtur was designed around the middle of the sixties by the Roman architect Andrea Nonis, who worked mostly in Algeria and died in 2017. Its discothèque is located on the tennis court and compensates for the fact that the Villaggio is today the only presence on the otherwise uninhabited island. In front is a beach of white sand that looks almost Caribbean. Beyond this is the Isolotto Roma, a small island that acts as a breakwater and recalls the sinking of the eponymous ship following a German attack just after the armistice of September 1943. The architecture of the Villaggio is well designed; it is in a rectilinear, rationalist style, quite the opposite of the expressionism used for the Hotel Cala di Volpe, dating from a few years earlier, whose situation in the landscape is comparable. When there were fewer boats passing through the channel than today, my brother and I used to swim to Santo Stefano in half an hour, accompanied by a small support boat. Every so often we all went with our Zodiac to the Valtur for an aperitif; my father would order a gin and tonic, my mother a glass of *vermentino*, and we kids a tomato juice; at the entrance you exchanged lire for a local currency that consisted of multicolored chips; it was considered a den of unconventional counterculture. Its dark brown volumes brake up the imposing structure (300 rooms, about 750 residents) into a series of parallelepipeds and prisms, making it look like a pre-Cubist picture by Cézanne or Derain. The attention paid to the relationship with the landscape prevents it turning into a conjuring trick of camouflage. The repetitive rooms are arranged in a line and have flat roofs, creating the effect of row houses set on a slight slope; the communal spaces are squeezed in a building in the form of a ziggurat near the beach.

If the resort of Santo Stefano should be considered a village, then Stazzo Pulcheddu should be considered a resort. Stazzo Pulcheddu is located a few kilometers inland of Palau and was founded toward the end of the seventies as a resort made up of private houses and a hotel, built to a design by Ponis. In those years a new geographical situation was emerging out of the attempts to extend the breadth of the coastal strip farther inland. Around a decade later came the wave of agritourism facilities, which established a connection with the Sardinian countryside rather than the sea. On the gentle slopes of a plot of land facing north Ponis, who up until then had mostly built private houses on steep and rocky sites close to the sea, realized at Pulcheddu a multifaceted urban composition comprising different types of accommodation for middle-class clients who wanted to be able to see the sea but were content with a platonic view from a distance. Sea Ranch, an integrated project of architecture and landscaping designed by MLTW in northern California in the sixties, was for Ponis an example to follow, with its environmentalist ambitions and predominant use of wood. The seasonal religious sanctuaries typical of the interior of Sardinia were another source of inspiration (for example, those of San Salvatore di Sinis near Oristano, Nostra Signora dell'Annunziata near Bitti or Santi Cosma e Damiano near Mamoiada), pushing him toward something whose beauty was rooted in simplicity, repetition, and rationality, and in which the seasonal nature of its use would not constitute a problem. Whether empty or crowded during the festivities, these sanctuaries still retain their quality, rooted in proportions, universality and absence of rhetoric; at once secular and sacred, they sit apparently isolated in a deserted landscape but in reality are at the center of networks, routes, and horizons that once made up the life of the countryside, as Giuseppe Dessì relates in his books. Thus at Pulcheddu each row house has been contrived to appear isolated, and is provided with its own *hortus conclusus*; the vistas and slopes make the most of the three-dimensional character of the landscape. Unlike on the Costa Smeralda—with which Ponis never wanted to get involved and has maintained a silent dispute from a distance—the slopes of Pulcheddu have never become true gardens but have for the most part remained natural scrub.

Two guests come back in the evening after having been out all day.

—"How did it go?"

—"It was hot, the beaches were packed. Slow queues at every roundabout. We had to walk in the sun and the restaurants only so-so. I don't know why we did it. It's August after all."

—"Where did you go?"

—"Toward and beyond Santa Teresa, in the opposite direction to the Costa Smeralda. You told us we'd find lots of beaches there."

—"Well, I thought you ought to see something more of Sardinia, instead of just lazing around in comfort here."

—"The whole day we've been prisoners of a series of paradises, but many of them ruined by you planners and architects."

—"I liked the estuary of the Liscia, fresh and salt water together. At Capo Testa on the isthmus a village has sprung up over the years that they forgot to design. Beyond Santa Teresa it's beautiful but windy, almost impossible to swim."

—"The resort of Marmorata defies imagination. And Costa Paradiso is hell on earth."

—"Well, you can't have everything. Beautiful places are usually the ones you can't get to. Those that are easy to reach generally lose their beauty. Now that you're back at base camp, take a rest and go for a swim."

—"I'm worn out, I feel as if I've just been through a washing machine. Being back here seems almost too good to be true. This place is a fantastic fragment that has nothing to do with the rest. You need to go away just in order to come back."

—"You're only saying these things to please me, just because you're leaving tomorrow."

At an auction I once bought a black-and-white photograph by Domenico Riccardo Peretti Griva, a Piedmontese photographer, magistrate and antifascist. Mine was the only bid; better that way. The picture intrigued me as soon as I saw it because it is small in size, somewhat out-of-focus, and impressionistic; nothing clearly defined or easy to identify. It's as if the whole surface were covered with powder in different tones, in which it is even possible to recognize grains of silver. Underneath, next to Peretti Griva's almost legible signature in pencil, the title: Rude Sardegna ("Rugged Sardinia"). The photograph is of a typical Sardinian landscape; and it could not be of anywhere else. It dates from the 1930s. All around, an elegant frame drawn in pencil with mathematical precision using a ruler and a set square, as was once the custom; the sheet of yellowish paper is much bigger than the print. Over half the image is taken up by the sky, with a few whitish clouds. I imagine being there: it is early September, mid-afternoon, and

Domenico Riccardo Peretti Griva, *Rude Sardegna*, ca. 1930s.
Archive Sebastiano Brandolini.

still hot. The sun is high, there are no shadows to be seen, the colors are muted, the air and the meadows have the look of a semidesert, no trace of water, of cows or goats in the environs, total silence apart from the song of the cicadas. The horizon is at once near and far; there are no troughs or ridges, just undulations. We feel like keeping still. There is nothing particular or surprising to look at, because it is a common situation, if not an ordinary one. We would like and not like to be there. Something makes the place slightly disquieting; we don't know what is behind us, how far away the nearest village is, and whether there is a road or not. What are we doing here? The photograph is a carefully balanced pictorial composition that contains three symbols—or perhaps we ought to call them idols—of the Sardinian landscape, which had always been there and probably still are today. As well as being an enthusiast for and expert on modern techniques of shooting and printing, Peretti Griva regarded photography as an extension of painting, in contrast to the modernist photography of those years which wanted to cut any ties with the past. The three idols have been chosen with care and thought: a granite rock in the foreground, a twisted and asymmetrical wild olive tree just behind it, and a nuraghe in a good state of preservation in the background. The image, at once romantic and analytical, offers us a bit of geology, a bit of botany, and a bit of archeology; it brings together three formally different scientific disciplines, linking them conceptually through the echoes and odors that can be sensed in the air. The patches of lichen on the granite, the leaves of the wild olive ruffled by the wind, and the megalithic front of the nuraghe are all described with deliberate imprecision. It is just this imprecision that makes the photograph so realistic and accurate.

I would like to contrast this single photograph with a series of pictures taken in the same years by another gentleman from Piedmont, Vittorio Sella, mountaineer, explorer, and nephew of Quintino, three-time Minister of Finance of the Kingdom of Italy. We know the place where they were taken, the locality I Piani, a few kilometers north of Alghero; here in fact is located the great Sella & Mosca wine estate, with its orderly network of farm roads that have an air of the Po Valley. Little has changed since then, except that just outside the boundaries of the property a profusion of

Vittorio Sella, panoramic view of the Sella & Mosca vineyards, Alghero, Sardinia, 1920.
© Fondazione Sella.

small sheds, houses, villas, and agritourism ventures have sprung up over the years. Sella's images document a project and a family asset, and the transformation of the investment in I Piani in a modern, productive, Savoy military sense. Looking at his photographs in chronological order (he went there at least eight times between 1914 and 1939), we can see that in the beginning the stony fields were grazed by flocks of sheep, and that they were then gradually dug up, cleared of stones, plowed, irrigated, and planted with vines. At the center a complex of farm buildings was constructed, a sort of *castrum* with blocks up to three stories high surrounded by the shade of leafy trees (maritime pine and eucalyptus), together with a small church and a garden for the proprietors. It feels like somewhere in the Piedmontese province of Biella. The pictures of the landscape that Vittorio Sella took with his cumbersome view camera, traveling around Sardinia by car—something few others could afford to do in those years—are for the most part in a long horizontal format, what would be called ultra-wide-angle today. They are idol-free images. The format lends itself to the spatiality and slow cadence without the marked relief of the Sardinian topography, which is neither "flat" nor "hilly" nor "mountainous," but something else, an eccentric mix of all three. With his eye accustomed to high altitudes, Sella gave the rugged and lunar scenery of Sardinia the same heroic dignity as the iconic images he produced of some of the world's principal mountain ranges: the Alps, the Caucasus, the Karakorum, Alaska.

Peretti Griva and Sella are just two of the many photographers who between 1850 and 1950 were drawn by the unique character of this island, and who included it in their reportages, at the dawn of modernity and between the various wars that were fought in Europe. Three luscious volumes published by Ilisso of Nuoro present a century and more of photographic views of Sardinia from the outside world. Coming from different countries, many photographers took an anthropological approach, painting a collective and substantially homogeneous portrait of the island from a social and cultural perspective: proud expressions on the lined faces of worn-out people who understandably smiled rarely, caps and headscarves concealing their hair; grazing and livestock, subsistence agriculture; basic items (what we would call "handicrafts" today); the almost total absence of writing; ragged children and houses built of mud; village fairs and religious festivities; costumes; transhumance, the interiors of houses furnished with the strictly indispensable; poverty everywhere; an atmosphere of basic survival. Cagliari and Sassari were the only two cities, the rest were villages, i.e., just houses abutting one against the other. Unable to believe their eyes, the photographers were hypnotized by the exceptional nature of what they found, and felt the thrill of being able to turn back the clock of history. Some (including Besso, Villani, Aragozzini, the architect Giuseppe Pagano, and the Austrian Suschitzky) focused on the trauma and hopes generated by the arrival of modern technology and the difficulty it had taking root in the poor geography of the Sardinian territory: mines, industries, electric power plants, the fight against malaria, the railroad lines, dams, and bridges. Between 1850 and 1950, none of these photographers seems to have noticed the presence of the sea, or to have been visually intrigued or interested by it. There are a few photographs of fishing boats in the harbors of Cagliari and Alghero, or of the islands of La Maddalena and Caprera (fundamental here, the presence of Giuseppe Garibaldi and relics of his life), or the landscape photos of the brothers Erminio and Vittorio Sella, but overall what stands out is the total absence of the coast and the sea. In 1913–1914 Vittorio Alinari photographed a bloody slaughter of tuna at Porto Torres. Around the same time, the Swiss photographer Werner Bischof (who worked for *Du* and *Life* before joining Magnum) captured the long beach of Funtanamare against the sun with a donkey in the foreground. In short, up until seventy years ago the two thousand kilometers of Sardinia's coastline, in addition to being extremely difficult to access from the land except at the few ports or industrial facilities, were not even part of its human geography, and still less of its cultural identity.

In the 1950s, as tourism took off and paid vacations became a civil right, its (geographical, anthropological, and folkloristic) imagery, which had previously been shaped in part by photography, was institutionalized. In 1950 the ESIT (Ente Sardo Industrie Turistiche) was set up, with its own promotional magazine. In 1956 Walt Disney produced the documentary *Sardinia*, made by Ben Sharpsteen, a director who would go on to win two Oscars in 1959;

the well-known Sardinian writer Giuseppe Dessì described the documentary as something that had "another sense of time, a different pace." In 1959 the regional government of Sardinia founded the ISOLA (Istituto Sardo Organizzazione Lavoro Artigianale), which under the direction of Eugenio Tavolara and Ubaldo Badas set out to promote, and create new forms of handicraft, and which won the gold medal at the Milan Triennale the same year. My parents may have visited this exhibition or heard about it. Although outside observers continued to show most interest in the more internal and introverted areas of the island, with their ancestral and apparently immutable customs, Sardinia as a whole was eager for progress in those years, and progress brought losses and gains, both prosperity and discontent. Even today, in the island's publicity for its tourist industry, the message is still being repeated that here time has magically come to a stop. The idols, like the masks, the nuraghes, the centuries-old wild olive trees and the architecture of the Costa Smeralda, are a demonstration of this.

For much of the nineteenth century, not even Sardinian painting showed much interest in the landscape, whether inland or on the coast. We should not be too surprised at this, given that Sardinia had had little to do with the classical world and was too remote to be a stop on the Grand Tour, and that paintings of Italian landscapes were almost always backdrops to scenes from history or great artistic monuments. In the 1800s Sardinian painters devoted themselves not to this subject, but chiefly to celebratory portraits of well-known personalities, showy altarpieces, and the odd anecdotal scene of limited historical significance. Along with busts in white marble, sculptors executed numerous sepulchral monuments in the style of Canova, blending religion and public spirit to the point where they became indistinguishable. When there were landscapes to be filled in within the background of the paintings, they were mostly generic, resembling those of the Alps or the Castelli Romani. Only toward the end of the century, in the wake of the success of prints and the growing popularity of photography, did some painters, intrigued by the peculiarities of the Sardinian landscape, begin to study and represent it, applying the verist lesson of the Macchiaioli, active a few years earlier in the Maremma region of Tuscany. The Sardinian pictures of the

Caprera - Casetta costruita personalmente dal
Generale Garibaldi -

House of Giuseppe Garibaldi, Caprera—postcard.
Archive Sebastiano Brandolini.

Piedmontese painter Giovanni Battista Quadrone (1844–1898) stand out: some of their framing seems to have been inspired by photography, showing that there were exchanges of ideas as well as rivalries between the two artistic disciplines. He painted scenes of hunting (of which he was an enthusiast), religious processions through deserted landscapes, people in costume, farming and pastoralism, buildings devoid of decoration, skies swept by the Maestrale, the textures of tobacco-colored land burnt by the sun. He was also intrigued by the bizarre forms of some granite boulders, although he was unable to convey their actual dimensions.

My parents never made Sardinia the object of their existential desires, but just one part of it, the coast facing the Arcipelago de La Maddalena. They neither knew nor were interested in the rest of the island. They turned their noses up at its ethnic and folkloristic peculiarities, considering them banal. They had seen enough of masks, dances, and costumes in South Africa. My mother thought the bronze statuettes of the Nuragic age to be primitive in comparison with what was being produced in the same centuries in Egypt or on Crete. They saw Sardinia as a desert, and paradoxically this is what made them want to be there. For my generation things are different. Although a lot of the tourists who frequent the Costa Smeralda today would not even be able to point to it on a map, many Sardinian sites have now been given the status of ancient monuments. Today Sardinia should be thought of as an organic whole. Its sea cannot be separated from its interior; it is a blue rind that cannot be peeled away from its gray innards. The boundary of this almost rectangular island, with its two large gulfs in the north and the south, is made of the same stuff as its heart. Many people arriving from the big cities of Europe are looking for something profound and intimate in that heart, something that is not fatuous. Many assign growing importance to the Sardinian diet and lifestyle. Books of real quality are being published and fascinating museums opening in unexpected places. Fellow architects coming from the far ends of the Earth speak to me of this with wonder, asking how all this is still possible.

Every corner of the Italian territory, be it a harbor, a mountain, a city or a small town, has over the last two centuries been the theater of war and conflict, and has seen troops pass through.

The partisan war of resistance was fought in much of Northern Italy, especially in the Alps and the Apennines. Commemorative plaques, statues, and cemeteries can be found almost everywhere, but are rare here in Sardinia. The island contributed to the First World War through the feared Sassari Brigade, which distinguished itself on the plateaus of Karst and Asiago. During the Second World War Sardinia served as an air and naval base—it was even called the aircraft carrier of the *Mare Nostrum*—and was bombed in 1942–1943 by the Allies (Cagliari in particular, but also Olbia, Sassari, Alghero, and Macomer). On September 8, 1943, when Italy surrendered unconditionally to the Allies following the signing of the Armistice of Cassibile, 32,000 German soldiers withdrew from Sardinia to Corsica, where they then fought against the French. The conditions were not created for a partisan resistance in Sardinia, and this according to some historians explains why the parties of the left had no particular success here after the war. On the coast the war was present, but there was no fighting; inland there was little awareness of the war, except on the part of the young men who were sent to the Balkans or to Russia, often ignorant of geography and without any understanding of where they were really going. Under its rough exterior and looking past its reputation for quarrelsomeness, Sardinia appears to be a peaceful island, one in which history and the passage of time are not commemorated through vestiges or monuments. There are few buildings—public or private—that have acquired the status of celebratory architecture. In the view of some, Sardinia is actually a land without architecture. The nuraghes, the countryside churches, the religious centers, the town halls, the *stazzi*, and the settlements themselves are mostly anti-iconic and neutral, there to accomplish a basic need, not to get themselves noticed. The people often seem indifferent, proud and laconic, and in their refusal to be bowed down by the incidents of everyday existence appear impervious to the flow of time, whether that of the past or the future. The inexorability of destiny seems to throw its pall over many things here. The ideas of new and old are of only relative importance; it matters little if the new seems old (like the buildings of Porto Cervo) or the ancient seems modern (like the giants' tombs). The grindstone of time is democratic. Even the landscape—portrayed in such different ways by Peretti Griva and Vittorio Sella—is seen as a fatality, and it is not always easy to tell whether a piece of land has been abandoned or not, who its owner might be, and what it could be used for. For this reason, the vineyards look out of keeping with the rest, with their tidy rows hugging the contours, leafless in the winter and separated by bare earth in the summer. They are an expression of productive agriculture, for winemaking is no longer a subsistence activity. The drystone walls, partially the result of the 1823 Edict of Enclosures and the related land reform, no longer mark the boundaries of properties, for they have lapsed into oblivion and pointlessness. Reservoirs and dams, constructed on the island's main rivers, ensure the supply of water and produce electric power; their surreal turquoise color makes them look like mirages, triggering short-circuits with the thirsty slopes surrounding them. The Sardinian landscape reflects precisely and faithfully the climatic, demographic, economic, and social changes under way, but at its own pace.

A few kilometers southwest of Nuoro, the village of Orani— 3,000 inhabitants—is set lethargically on the side of a mountain and boasts a small museum designed by the globalized American architectural firm Skidmore Owings & Merrill (SOM). The museum is dedicated to the work of native sculptor Costantino Nivola, a surname that can be pronounced in three different ways: with the accent on the "o" in Sardinian, on the "i" in Italian, and on the "a" in French. Nivola was born in Orani in 1911 (his father was a mason), worked as an art director for Olivetti, lived for a while in Paris, and fled Italy in 1938 following the introduction of the racial laws, having married that same year the wealthy American Jew of German origin Ruth Guggenheim. He lived practically the rest of his life at East Hampton on Long Island and was an active member of the artistic and academic community in New York, collaborating with many good modernist architects. He invented the sculptural technique of sandcasting: "First of all I put wet sand in wooden molds and start making drawings. The tools of my trade can be anything: a knife, a shell, my thumb. When the drawing is complete, I pour plaster of Paris over the form of sand and when the plaster is dry my sculpture is ready, and has a beautiful fuzzy surface of sand."

This simple idea, which apparently came to him while playing with his children on the beach, reflects his Sardinian spirit in its immediacy and unpretentious archaism. Dessì has aptly described Sardinia as a "a piece of moon." Nivola was also a sculptor of objects that resemble idols and amulets, at once Nuragic and avant-gardist: ancient forms that can be found in many of the products of the island's crafts, such as jewelry, farming implements, children's toys, boxes, household furniture, woven baskets, clothing, and loaves of bread. Anyone visiting the Museo Nivola can sense the presence of a magnetic field that indissolubly binds work and place and will probably wonder if his sand-casting creations are not also models of landscapes, with their slopes, differences in height, fields, plateaus, and retaining walls. At Ulassai, in the nearby region of Ogliastra, Nivola made an exquisite sound fountain. In the center of Nuoro he designed Piazza Sebastiano Satta, an urban space that resembles a landscape peopled by disquieting idols carved out of granite from the nearby Monte Ortobene. In the seventies Nivola encouraged the people of Orani to adopt a parsimonious way of life and resist the easy enrichment that at the time seemed to inevitably accompany tourism in the age of globalization. To his fellow villagers, who were at last managing to emerge from an atavistic and age-old poverty linked to farming, he explained that tradition is important, and that owning a car was not something of fundamental importance. Someone asked him why he had not even provided a drinking fountain in Piazza Satta; his response, sour and ironic, was that he had had to shave with mineral water that very morning, as there was no running water in Orani.

Certain places—or perhaps objects—in the interior of Sardinia have left such a deep impression on my mind that I cannot rid myself of them, becoming obsessions that give me pleasure and prompt reflections. For us obligatory positivists of the twenty-first century, there is something enigmatic and incomprehensible about these objects. They oscillate between architecture, archeology, geology, and landscape, but do not belong to any of these categories; as soon as we think we've found a plausible classification, we are assailed by doubts and qualifications. It matters little exactly what they are, when they date from and what use

219

26843 - NUORO - Giardini e Casa di Grazia Deledda

House of Grazia Deledda, Nuoro—postcard.
Archive Sebastiano Brandolini.

they might be to us; what is important is their enigmatic character and the fact that, being hard to find, they offer us the thrill of discovery. For me Grazia Deledda's house in Nuoro is one of these places; it has a broad staircase, a back garden, and the atmosphere of a place of work. I find the pre-Nuragic temple-altar of Monte d'Accoddi with its Mesopotamian flavor miraculous, a physical mediation between earth and sky, and yet absent from many of the guidebooks. The Nuragic village of Tiscali, constructed inside a gigantic sinkhole, is an almost inaccessible hideaway, hard to describe. The temporary village of San Salvatore, near the pond of Cabras, encapsulates the essence of a religious community that assigns importance to both the spiritual and the practical. None of these things is based on a rational design and a sense of communicable beauty, in contrast to the works that are found on the other large Italian island in the Mediterranean, Sicily, permeated by clarity and classical culture.

The interior of Sardinia is easier to describe in words (i.e., from a literary viewpoint) than through images (i.e., figuratively). Its millenary figurative iconoclasm, in part due to its geographical location, forges a curious tie with modernity. Its language and its legends and traditions have caught the interest of ethnologists, linguists, and writers. D. H. Lawrence paid a fleeting visit with his wife Frieda, nicknamed Queen Bee, in 1921, and wrote a short book about it. No one, I would say, has written of it with the same empathy and correctness of language as Salvatore Satta, whose descriptions are more faithful and accurate than any picture by a verist painter: his language cuts like a scalpel and dissects the crude reality of things, which is sometimes hard to accept. His masterpiece, the diary-novel *Il giorno del giudizio*, was brought out posthumously in 1977 by a publisher specializing in legal matters, and later by Adelphi. It relates the life led by the inhabitants of Nuoro and by the author's acquaintances and relatives in the years of his childhood, in a welter of memories and reconstructions rooted in psychology and sociology, accounts of jealousies, quarrels, and petty vengeances in the bosom of a family trapped in the rooms of its townhouse. The gloomy and stifling city is the theater in which peasants and shepherds, notables and profiteers, technological progress and ultra-conservatism, Church and State clash to the point of canceling each other out and making the whole of existence fester. The interior spaces, the buildings, the cities, and the landscape constitute the inescapable stages on which the events of the book are played out.

In my youth I was infatuated with archeology, thinking it to be something romantic and adventurous, as it was portrayed in the popular books of the German writer C. W. Ceram. My enthusiasm has lasted, although it is now filtered through architecture. In the early seventies, we once went to Sardinia for Christmas. Early one morning my father and I set off on a visit to three ancient monuments on the west coast, each an expression of a different civilization: the Losa nuraghe at Abbasanta, the Phoenician-Roman colony of Tharros, and the early-Christian church of San Giovanni in Sinis. Crossing the island diagonally we got a sense of its size, the vastness of its horizons and its confused topography. Once I reached the age of fourteen, I started to take day trips on my Ciao moped, venturing a bit farther each time to the growing irritation of my mother, who saw these explorations as betrayals of herself and Porto Ulisse: I went as far as Monti, Tempio, and Oschiri and visited nuraghes, giants' tombs, dolmens, and small churches scattered without any apparent logic around the countryside, traveling along monotonous roads with little traffic, continuous ups and downs, and hardly any shade. I noted the scarcity, in villages and towns, of commercial enterprises and meeting places; in some there was nothing but a post office, a gas station, the barracks of the carabinieri, and a church with an attached oratory and soccer pitch. I realized that here silences were deeper than elsewhere, because they were part of interpersonal communication; here, remaining mute meant something, and keeping quiet did not necessarily produce silences. I thought that it was a civilization apart. I saw that its territory was made up of tones of gray, and how little color there was. On 1,400-meter-high Monte Limbara, I discovered it could be cool even in summer. With the passing of time, the significance of these little expeditions became clear to me: I was tracing the lines of force—physical and mental—that would connect the house (which forty years later was to become mine) to the rest of the island.

This phase of exploration continued until the age of sixteen, when I set off with a friend, again on my moped, to drive all the way round Sardinia in four days, a distance of 800 kilometers. The length of the stages and the heat meant there was little time left for archeology. Leaving from Palau, we camped the first night at Arbatax, the second on the island of Sant'Antioco without even giving Cagliari a glance, the third at Oristano; we got back home sunburned, full of aches and pains. From these adolescent adventures I have kept the photographs, and the desire to go on traveling around by car with the air conditioning on and a map in my hand, but no precise goals. I will never stop being surprised at how big and sparsely populated Ichnusa is, and how impermeable it remains to tourism: Ichnusa is the name the ancient Greeks gave to the island, *ichnos* being the word for the footprint it resembles. I admire its tenacious indifference to the outside world. One weekend, in the center of Oristano, my wife Alba and I were looking for a place to have lunch, but there were no passersby to ask and no signs. On one street we noticed some unusual movement, and so we plucked up courage and entered what looked like a private house. What was revealed to us, like an apparition, was a large restaurant, probably the best in Oristano, filled with mostly silent locals who stared at us, asking with their eyes who we were and where we came from. We said our greetings and, thirsty and hungry, sat down at one of the few free tables, over which had just been spread a white cloth.

A t the time, I don't know if my father and his partner in the purchase of the land, the engineer Piero Paccagnella from Conegliano Veneto, asked themselves whether there was going to be any water. They probably did, being provident people. The fact of the shortage of water all over the Mediterranean basin could not have escaped them. But, caught up in their enthusiasm and sense of adventure, they may have underestimated the problem. For them, the absence of difficulties would have meant no adventure either. Nonetheless, for about fifteen years the supply of water was the main problem, a permanent headache. We used very little, and what did reach the house was often the color of mud, or rust. In *Cosima*, the autobiographical novel published in 1937, Grazia Deledda spoke of the importance of water in the life of her family at their home in Nuoro:

On the sink there always stood a copper pot full of water drawn from the well in the courtyard, and on a bench the clay amphora with drinking water, laboriously brought from the spring a long way from the built-up area. Water was a problem then, and it was doled out drop by drop in the summer; unless a good downpour arrived to fill the tub located under the drainpipe from the roof: and yet the most diligent cleaning, done with no water, gave the whole house a pleasant air.

This is our story of that primary commodity, water. Initially, a well was drilled in a position halfway between the first two houses, Casa Brandolini and Casa Paccagnella, at the point where their respective roads of access divided and where the water running down from the Orso converged and collected. In winter and spring, the season of the rains, a foaming torrent sometimes forms here, but only for a few hours. Between the well and our house the ground first rises and then falls. A line was built and fitted with a pump that lifted the water to three Eternit tanks, located at the highest point, from which it then flowed by gravity down to our faucets. To the disapproval of my mother, who thought it in bad taste, Paccagnella had a mock nuraghe constructed around the well and pump that is still there today, although overrun by vegetation. Things did not turn out to be as simple as was hoped, since from mid-July there was little water in the well and it filled up with mud. Unable to draw, the pump suffered damage and had to be replaced repeatedly. When rust-colored water started to come out of the faucet, it was necessary first to go and check if the Eternit tanks were full and then to the well, to try to see (with a lighter or flashlight) whether there was any water left. If there was none in either of the tanks or the well, we were in serious trouble. All this was trying, since the house would be full of friends and children, who needed to wash themselves at the end of the day. The problem was not drinking water, which could be bought in Palau or collected directly from the many fountains supplied by springs along the roads, but domestic water, needed to fill the baths, wash the dishes, and mop the floors, as well as to water every evening the pot of basil given to us by Alberto Ponis. At a certain point a

House with its water tank.
Photographer Alba Gallizia/Archive Sebastiano Brandolini.

frantic campaign of exploration was launched to find places in the vicinity where other wells could be dug, at any point where there was a natural valley or traces of moisture in the ground. More water had to be found.

Figures seemingly out of antiquity arrived from the Sardinian hinterland, men who sweated profusely but did not fear the heat, dowsers equipped with instruments resembling wands that started to rattle when the humidity increased and that were able to detect the mythical presence of water. At the end of the day they told us exactly where we should dig, the precise point. Then a path was cut through the scrub, suitable machinery arrived, a well was drilled, and everyone watched with jubilation as a few hundred liters of water flowed out. For us, it was something more valuable than gasoline, but it was only enough to last a few days, at most a week. The following year, the frantic search was resumed, but with a bit more skepticism. There are still some who claim, with confidence, that at Capo d'Orso there is plenty of water in the fissures of the granite, and that it's there all year round, but you need to have patience, dig deeper, and believe in the spirit of nature, as well as a bit of luck. In those years the water main that would shortly be installed under the road linking Palau with Capo d'Orso did not yet exist and so there did not seem to be any alternative to wells. Then, when the main was built at the beginning of the eighties, Porto Ulisse diligently did its part and prepared to lay its pipe under the dirt road, so that it would be possible to make a connection. At this point the two original houses on the property were about to become four. In the end the connection was never made, as the utility company could not guarantee supply in the summer months, since the new seasonal villages and hotels under construction at Capo d'Orso would be given precedence.

It was then that we realized the only possible solution to the longstanding problem of the supply of domestic water was to build tanks, one for each house, to be regularly filled by a water truck. The concept was taken from the reservoirs that dot the mountainous heart of Sardinia (fed by the Liscia, Tirso, Coghinas, and Flumendosa rivers), lakes that heave into sight suddenly from the car, almost frightening presences. Four tanks (one per house) were the obvious solution. Water, it should be remembered, was needed when it did not rain, that is from April to October, when the sun shines. It ought to have been enough to observe, in the courtyard of the little *stazzo* at Capo d'Orso where Rosa Filigheddu lived, the dozens of buckets, drums, basins, tubs, cans, and pots scattered all over the place to collect water in the winter, for us to realize that we were certainly not the first to encounter what was an old problem. It would have been sufficient to notice, just above the Saline, a small architectural complex made up of a *stazzo* with a pitched roof and a tank in which to store water, both of the same size, to realize that in the summer the volume of water needed is as great as the volume of the house. The second house built by my father—which he then sold—was equipped with a large underground tank from the outset, constructed to catch the water of the stream that runs down from the Orso in the winter. In the same years a tank was built for our first house too, just under the parking area, where it is still in use; in the summer it is filled regularly by Mannoni, who delivers the water early in the morning with a truck, after drawing it from the Liscia at Porto Pozzo. The old system (wells, pump, Eternit tanks, and pipes), long disused and never reassessed, will delight future archeologists of the age of tourism.

Mannoni used to descend silently by the path in the heavy boots that he wore all year round, seat himself laconically at the big table under the portico, stare impassively at the sea which he had never touched and which Sardinians had for centuries considered an impassable limit, and wait for my father to come down around eight o'clock in order to chat a while. They respected and understood each other, even though they came from worlds that were poles apart. My father knew that Mannoni (dark complexion, a deeply lined face, a bushy moustache of a shade somewhere between white and yellow) would be there waiting for him, and that he would prefer beer to coffee, and so did not even ask him.

—"Good morning Mannoni, so how are things?"
—"*Ajò!* Well, I'm getting by ... Always beautiful here."
—"Beautiful, yes. It seems to me that there are more people around this year. A few more boats passing by than last year."

—"Hmm, some have already come, but not so many as other years ..."

—"Mannoni, we were looking for someone trustworthy to do some work around the house this winter. Anyone you might recommend?"

—"Hmm, I'll tell my cousin Pasquale, he'll know if anyone has the time. There's no hurry anyway ... eh?"

—"Another drop of beer ... Please, finish it ..."

—"*Ajò*, just a finger, up to here ..."

—"Do you think it's worth connecting to the water main they have laid up to Capo d'Orso, or should we carry on like this a few more years?"

—"Hmm, that'll be the day! There's never any shortage of water in the Liscia, and there's always someone ready to bring it here, but the road is bad and the truck almost can't make it anymore, and the clutch ... It needs some gravel ..."

—"And the family, everyone well back home?"

—"Let's not complain. We've enlarged the petrol station and installed a car wash. People are already coming ... A lot of foreigners ..."

—"Good, good. So we'll talk again next week, when the tank will be almost empty. Then we'll be leaving, and afterward Sebastiano is coming with his family and their little boy, Martino."

As for drinking water, we reckon on two to three liters per person per day. In the early years we didn't buy bottles of water because in the house there was a good stock of plastic jerry cans, to be filled every time we went to Palau at a public drinking fountain near the level crossing where people were always standing in line. One year at the beginning of the seventies, it rained in late spring. At the bottom of a little valley next to the house and close to the sea, a stream formed that ran until the end of June; then the flow turned into a dribble, every day a little less until all that remained were traces of moisture, before the thing dried up entirely. It's a great feeling to get fresh water directly from the landscape. Today we buy many packages of plastic bottles containing still and sparking water from the supermarket. When a summer thunderstorm breaks, sheets of water cascade in front of the arches from the broad roof of the house, which has no gutters or drainpipes. We wait under the portico in the dry and are treated to an unexpected Eliasson-like performance; if the wind is blowing, the water gets driven under the portico, but that matters little. Some say this water that arrives free of charge from the sky should not be wasted but collected. Yet I hear nothing but complaints from those who have constructed houses with flat roofs in order to collect rainwater, as it is always too little to meet the needs for the whole summer.

Then there is the drag of our garbage. Owing to the house's isolation, this has seen a succession of intricate and contradictory solutions over the years. What we used to do makes us shudder today, and if we did it again we would end up in front of a judge. Environmentalism, in the sense of a collective responsibility, is a recent phenomenon. The amount of waste and garbage that we once produced was considerable: the house was almost always full of hungry and pleasure-loving guests and friends, and this meant a massive daily shopping run; the bill with the small stores in Palau was settled in a lump sum at the end of the season; we never went to the Friday market and there was no supermarket. Many plastic and paper bags and wooden crates were brought down from the parking area to the house, but not much garbage was carried in the opposite direction. The instructions were clear: produce as little as possible, dispose of as much as possible of that in situ, and aim for self-sufficiency. There was a metal incinerator, whose essential and archetypal form—a cylinder on four legs, surmounted by a cone from which sprouted a chimney that was also cylindrical—would today recall some of the still lifes drawn by Aldo Rossi in those same years. Here we burned plastic, paper, and wood, because from our proto-environmentalist perspective throwing these materials into the sea would have polluted it, a sin that would have gone against our civic conscience. Almost every evening, a little before sunset, when the sea grew calm, we went out with *Caramella* to a point in the middle of the channel and dumped the glass and tin cans, which would end up in the dark at the bottom of the sea, and the organic leftovers like fruit, vegetables, mussel shells, and pieces of fish and cheese rind. After all, the ships did the same, we had seen them with our very eyes. Our spartan philosophy told us that this would be of benefit to the ecosystem, especially to the birds and fish. Sometimes, regrettably, the currents would wash up our own garbage on our own rocks, and we didn't like that at all.

Then the dumpsters arrived and shortly afterward the system of trash separation and collection. Our steel incinerator was eaten away by rust, and with it went our shameful habit of throwing our garbage in the sea. Dumpsters were located at four points along the road between Palau and Capo d'Orso, and in the summer they overflowed. People were starting to become aware of the problem posed by waste, from the hygienic, economic, and aesthetic perspective. In 1973 in Naples everyone was alarmed by an epidemic of cholera, eradicated in part thanks to the organizational efficiency of the American troops stationed in the city. Two dumps were created in the vicinity of Palau. Points were also set up for the collection and disposal of the bulky waste produced by tourists, whose number by now exceeded that of residents by a factor of more than ten. We threw away old and rusty metal furniture, damaged dinghies and rowboats, and unmentionable objects thrown up on the rocks by heavy winter sea. Today the dumpsters have gone too. Along the dirt road each of the four houses has its own garbage bins, and in summer these should in theory be emptied twice a week. The system for the disposal of waste in operation fifty years ago, in which each household had to dispose of its own waste, was conceptually correct, but the technology was not up to the task, and neither is it today. Maybe one day my pink house will become self-sufficient again.

Water and waste are part of logic and logistics, as are the telephone and the mail. Once we enjoyed our isolation even with regard to telecommunications. To call someone we would have to go to Palau, where there were three possibilities: we could go to the general and hardware store, where there was a pay phone, to the port, where there was a phone booth of the SIP (Società Italiana per l'Esercizio Telefonico), much used by the soldiers of the American military base, or to Ponis's studio, where we would be tolerated but told to be quick, as the telephone was needed for work. If there was no need to go to Palau for other things, we could just go to the bar at Capo d'Orso, which was closer, use the pay phone that was housed in a claustrophobic soundproof cabin, and have an ice cream. Things went on like this for years. It was only around 1990 that the house was given a telephone line of its own, not very good timing given that the era of cellphones started immediately afterward. The house lost a bit of its isolation, but not its solitude. Today, that phone line has gone too.

For years, the mail service was more vital than the phone, and was the umbilical cord connecting us to the mainland. Mail arrived regularly for us at the post office on Via Nazionale, and it was from there that we sent our letters and postcards. There was a permanent queue at the counter and poor ventilation, and the locals treated it as a place for conversation. For urgent matters (a last-minute change of plan, someone dying, final school grades, birthdays) we used telegrams, brittle sheets of yellow paper that had to be folded up like origami and opened carefully, onto which were glued strips of text without adjectives or punctuation, just the often repeated word *stop*, as in military dispatches. By the end of summer we would have sent or received dozens of telegrams. Postcards were used to send greetings and let people know we were alive and in good spirits; many were of the Orso (from the only position from which it is recognizable as a bear) or the pink and white beaches of the archipelago; we avoided those with Sardinian costumes and the ones whose subjects were of a blatantly sexual character. One year two postcards of our rocks went on sale, without anyone having asked our permission; gratified, we bought and sent many more than usual. Yasmin embellished them by adding a small drawing on the front or back; Brandolino made puns. The signatures were almost always illegible.

Then there is our story of gas. Before an electricity line was run alongside the Capo d'Orso road and an exclusive substation installed for the houses at Porto Ulisse, we did almost everything with gas. It arrived from Palau in 25-kilo cylinders, which were rolled down the path and carried back up on the shoulders when empty. Gas was used to cook, heat water, and run the refrigerator. There were two pairs of cylinders, housed in a brick structure outside the old kitchen, where there was always a slight smell of gas. When one pair ran out the other came into operation, and whoever was going into town would remember to order two more; and so it went on all summer. For lighting in the evening and at night, we used camping gas lamps or glass candleholders, depending on the wind, the amount of light required, and the desired atmosphere. Each of us had on our bedside table a *Lucciola*, an ingenious pocket flashlight consisting of a blue battery the size of the palm of a hand into which was inserted a bulb no bigger than a fingernail: a practical example of industrial design, but one that did not last long and easily oxidized.

Satta recounts how culturally revolutionary the arrival of lighting in the streets of Nuoro was in 1915:

> And what about street lighting? Certainly, with life changing as it does, they could not go on making their way down the street with flaming firebrands whenever they went out at night (and they went out only when necessary). In fact Don Priamo ... had concerned himself with this when he was mayor. That session remained memorable because the council wanted to limit oil lighting to moonless nights.

We too at Porto Ulisse, by connecting to the grid, adapted to a changing world.

I picture the future. Perhaps to meet its modest energy needs, the house will be equipped with three new technologies: solar panels on the roof, wind turbines on the rocks, and water turbines in the sea. It could become a hybrid of the romantic and the futuristic. If this were to happen, it would be a momentous transformation, considering that up to now the identity of the house has been associated with an almost total absence of technology.

I t has been quite an effort to talk about it, but also given me a degree of satisfaction. It's a holiday home that I love and cherish, but that has not always been the case. There have been a series of ups and downs in my relationship with the place and there continue to be, without any logic that I can grasp. There have been moments of love and loathing, of enthusiasm and indifference, of romanticism and introspection. There have been fasts and binges, periods of silence and outpourings. I have always been aware of its many strengths and its equally numerous flaws, to the point where I have often found myself reflecting on the strange fact that here strengths and flaws not only balance each other, but end up coinciding. It's not an ideal house that is good all year round, for a whole lifetime, for everyone. But is there any such thing as an ideal house, as Robert Louis Stevenson, man of the sea and son of a famous lighthouse engineer, once entitled one of his writings? It's a house made to bring out everything that is least comprehensible and most visceral in each of us. Every year, after spending a week or so on holiday here, I know that there always comes a time when, dejectedly, I am no longer able to make sense of my seasonal presence in this place. Then I wish I were somewhere else, in Croatia, in Greece, in the Canaries, or the Aeolian Islands, all places by the sea where I've never been. The house at Porto Ulisse is there to raise questions, rather than give answers. But in the end I also know that, every time I go there, I enjoy it profoundly, especially when (lying on my bed in the middle of the afternoon) I hear the echo of the waves breaking on the granite and am able to tell from the details of the sound they make whether the wind and the current are about to turn.

It is a house that many people don't cherish, or if they like it, it is only for a few days of holiday in the year, certainly not more than a week. The list of its defects is easy to draw up. It is isolated and you can have unpleasant encounters; it is far away from everything; you can't get close enough to it with a car; there is no room for a babysitter or other help in the house; it can only be used in the summer; it has no swimming pool and still less a beach; you have to be careful when making your way down to the sea; it is exposed to the Maestrale and the Ponente. I could go on: the bathrooms are small, the materials from which it is built are modest, it has no garden, it's not connected to the water main, it has no air conditioning, it's damp in the winter, the range of household appliances is basic, the wiring needs redoing, the bedrooms have no balconies, there is neither a television nor wi-fi. Some people say: "The problem is not just that that the house is getting old, but that it was poorly conceived from the outset!" Others add: "Irreparable errors have been made in its design!" The more malicious ask: "But sorry, aren't you an architect?" My father, in his old age, used to declare that it was a house for the young, and was convinced that everyone in their own lives should invent and realize their own places of reverie.

Owing to these flaws—which perhaps ought to be considered character traits—it has always been difficult to determine the salability and economic value of the house. Here it is not possible to apply the criteria of the real-estate market. What meaning does it have, with this light and these rocks, to assign a value per square meter, cubic meter, room, window, bed? Each of the house's defects undermines and confounds the price. When his health started to fail, my father wanted to sell it; he needed an injection of cash into his bank account. He was fed up with having to carry out every year the maintenance that an isolated house inevitably requires, and discovering every time that something was broken or not working properly. My parents chafed at the journeys, always lengthy whether by sea or air. They were no longer the same people who had made it a special place. No longer were they so nimble-footed and no longer did they feel the need to be mentally bound to such a demanding place. Things that had previously been to their taste now seemed insipid. The sale—or rather selling off—of the house would have been a liberation for them, from the economic and sentimental viewpoint. By the time they informed me, they'd already signed an agreement with a local real-estate agency to sell the house. I rebelled against this, feeling personally offended; there was a Chekhovian kind of generational conflict between us, as I argued that the house belonged spiritually to the whole family. The next day my father decided to call off the sale but taking me at my word got rid of the house anyway by making a donation of it in equal parts to his two sons and their respective wives.

Now I'm the one who's trying to sell it; history repeats itself in different tints and shades. It's not because of its faults, but because I make little use of it; luckily it doesn't require much maintenance. The various agencies I've contacted have come up with different estimates of its value, all just rough guesses seeing that the house lacks the basic requisites of the market. Some agencies have fallen in love with it as if it were a beautiful woman, to the point of saying that you can't put a price on the house as there's nothing comparable to it anywhere on the coast—from Olbia to Santa Teresa—not even in high-end resorts like Porto Cervo or Porto Rotondo. Other agencies say the exact opposite, almost as if they had come to an agreement between themselves to muddy the waters and confuse me: according to them the house is so full of problems that it's almost unmarketable; at the most it would be worth as much as two or three mediocre apartments in Palau, and the rocks and the closeness to the sea would in any case constitute an insurmountable snag. In either case, it seems I am the owner of an atypical property, and the house is an unsolvable equation.

There are many conventional villas that abide by the rules of the property market, designed and built to be attractive to as many people as possible, and there are particular houses that wouldn't know what to do with things like salability, success, and photogenic quality. A house is not a villa and a villa is not a house. In a house you live and stay, while in a villa you have fun and entertain. This doesn't mean you can't have fun in a house too; it is difficult to live in a villa as if it were a house. But there are exceptions. Andrea Palladio's La Malcontenta is at once a villa, a country house, and a farm, as its current owner Antonio Foscari has recounted in two books of a sentimental-autobiographical character; the first book describes the original functions of the spaces inside, the second the eccentric social life that went on in them last century. My house at Capo d'Orso has never been and will never become a villa, even though some people call it that, thinking I'll be gratified by this. There is an endless number of villas large and small in Sardinia, almost all of them built over the last fifty years, most of them comfortable as far as material needs are concerned, but wholly lacking with regard to spiritual ones. These villas maintain a vague relationship with the nature around them and with the landscape, contenting themselves with a neatly mown lawn and the odd exotic plant bought from the nursery. The word *villa* was once used to indicate the dimensions, proportions, and aura of a comfortable, airy, and symmetrical building, but in current Italian speech *villa*, *villetta*, and *villino* have become synonymous with modesty. Of the original noble idea of villa, be it Pompeiian, Venetian, British, or Corbusian, very little is left. In contrast, a house is a comfortable and practical place that is easy to live in, a bit like a good sweater or pair of shoes that you're always happy to wear.

In the end, my own sentimental autobiography really is about luxury. Just five years after my grandfather sold the massive Castello di Valmareno, my parents, in their early thirties, recreated for themselves an equally imaginary and unique place; they re-interpreted the luxury in which they had lived up until then to suit their own needs and taste. Ironically, what my parents thought of as a spartan holiday house fifty years ago has today risen to the status of an object of desire. In the meantime, the objects of desire built fifty years ago on the Costa Smeralda have been downgraded to basic commodities. What is true luxury today, in a world crammed with endless superfluities?

Some time ago, many years since my last visit, I returned to the archeological excavations at Herculaneum, by now part of the outskirts of Naples, on the Tyrrhenian coast and at the foot of the Vesuvius. Its one- or two-story houses, with their rooms almost all the same and without a precise function, laid out around well-proportioned courtyards through which water flows, with splendidly matched and assorted decorations and colors and no windows, seemed to me to be of an unparalleled luxury. What is true luxury today, where a basic necessity like architecture is concerned? Luxury does not mean a lot of space, but the right space. An immaterial light that creates plays of shadow, along with a breath of fresh air, has every right to be considered a luxury. A house set in a lunar landscape is also a luxury. When does being *without* something constitute a luxury? This question concerns our style of life and the places we live in—that is to say, architecture. My house is a luxury because its defects—meaning what it lacks—produce a new mental balance. It seems to me that my house satisfies Vitruvius's three principles of good architecture: *utilitas* (utility, functionality, necessity), *firmitas* (solidity, quality of materials, durability), and *venustas* (harmony, beauty, delight); thinking of my house as Vitruvian pleases me. I am also aware that my house can be regarded at once as modern (geometric layout, open plan, no decoration, empirical relationship with the context) and ancient (loadbearing walls, little technology, no insulation, hard to get to, easy to build). I find this temporal ambiguity reassuring.

Up at the parking place I meet an elegant woman from Central Europe, maybe interested in buying the house. She is wearing a swimming costume under her light dress. We speak in English; she intersperses a few words in Italian, and I do the same with the odd word in German. I start by asking her a straight question.

—"Are you an architect?"

—"No, I sell art. Up to now I've never owned a holiday house, indeed I'm allergic to the very idea, but my husband and children would really like one."

—"Well, this is a proper holiday house. How did you find out that it's for sale?"

—"I came across it by chance, and then tracked you down. I had a feeling that it's a house of a certain age, and that it belongs to yesterday's world, as Stefan Zweig said so aptly."

—"Stefan Zweig, of course. Well, mine is above all a modern house. It's environmental footprint is close to zero. You hardly even need electricity."

—"I have to ask: are there any skeletons in the closet?"

—"There are a lot of beautiful and ugly stories linked to the house, comedies and tragedies, that I haven't told before."

—"Such as?"

—"Deaths and injuries, fires, robberies, sudden flights by night, jealousies, insolvent tenants, prehistorical animals springing from nowhere, incomprehensible noises, momentous quarrels, bereavements, sea urchin spines, jellyfish, shipwrecks. Yesterday a hawk even flew into the house. A lady of easy virtue used it to entertain her clients … Things have happened here that you couldn't even begin to imagine."

—"In short, you're putting your life up for sale."

—"Perhaps the time has come. I'd say that the time has also come to go down the path, taking it easy, although I see you are wearing the right shoes, congratulations. This is the water tank and over there is the electrical cabinet."

—"It's clear that it's an existential place, one that troubles and doesn't console. It's a place made for going crazy!"

—"We stand now in the famous portico. You stay here, while I open up. Inside there's usually a slight smell of mold. Enjoy the arches, and if you like go down to the sea, you seem to already know the way."

—"You're selling a place, not a house."

—"For me a house is first of all a place. Only secondarily is a house a material thing. This is the difference between a work of architecture and a work of art."

—"And then a work of architecture can't be packed up and moved around, and it can't be stolen either. So, by having a house, you save a lot on insurance."

—"Let's go inside. We are now in the living room/kitchen, above are the three bedrooms."

—"The interior is more animated than I imagined. You can tell too that it wasn't designed by an architect. You'll have already realized that I don't think highly of your colleagues."

—"For that matter, neither do I. When the wind is blowing, endless currents of air are formed in the house, and you go where the current you like most is."

—"Thank you, now I will tell you. No, I'm not interested in your house. And you know why? Because in selling it you'd be committing a crime. The world today is going to the dogs because everything is assigned a financial value. But I'll give your name to some rich friends in Berlin, less moralistic than I am."

—"Do as you wish. You might want to take a swim; I assume you came for that too. You might change your mind after the swim."

During the roughly nine long winter months the house goes into hibernation, which means that almost nothing happens. For about ten years now there have been no more break-ins or thefts, although before that there was one practically every winter. Instead of thieves, wild boar ransack the ground in search of tubers. In winter bolete and meadow mushrooms sprout, in spring orchids and asphodels; downpours damage the road and turn the path into a waterfall; the wind displaces some of the roof tiles. The local fishermen arrive, kitted out with all their technological paraphernalia, angling from the shore for passing gilthead, dentex, and amberjack, using cuttlefish, sea cucumber, and garfish as bait. A few years ago, I came for a day in the winter to check on the execution of some minor maintenance work; I arrived at about ten o'clock and found a car in the parking place. On the rocks a fisherman had mounted eight rods in what looked like missile batteries, four on the artificial solarium to the east and four on the natural solarium to the west. I greeted him without reproaching him for having ignored the menacing signs saying "Private Property" and "Beware of the Dog," and he responded by asking who I was. I told him I was Brandolini, the owner. "Ah, you're Brandolini!" he said. "Then remember that you use the house for a couple of months a year, and I the other ten!" I smiled and said that he was absolutely right, and asked him to please take care of the house and the rocks, and to leave as few traces of his passage as possible. He was beaming because he had just hooked a large silver-colored dentex weighing 3–4 kilos, and let off steam by spinning yarns in the way all true fishermen do. He explained how he would have altered and enlarged the house if it were his and asked me if by chance I wanted to sell it, seeing that I used it so rarely. This time we both smiled. To show me that he knew something about luxury, he explained that he worked as a hotel barman: at the Cala di Volpe on the Costa Smeralda in the summer and at the Palace in St Moritz in the winter. I think he was telling the truth. Sardinians are people of honor and seldom lie.

I think the desire expressed by my parents to build a luxurious but primitive house turned out well in the end. In the winter the house is not so much damp as soaking wet, as it is barely touched by the rays of the sun. With the wind blowing from the northwest or the north, the salt spray of the sea reaches the portico. When it's time to shut up the house for the winter, the shutters get closed and the windows get left open, but this is not enough to keep it ventilated and dry. The floors, walls, and roof get saturated with water. Lighting a stove or turning on an electric heater in a room only makes the situation worse, because the air warms up but nothing dries, and so the rooms turn into Turkish baths, the window panes mist over and drops of condensation run over every surface. My parents were overoptimistic when they thought that a fireplace, located in the living room on the ground floor, would be enough to heat the house in spring and fall. The fireplace in the living room has now turned into a decorative object, the perfect place to put an aromatic sprig of *Helichrysum* or a piece of driftwood washed up on the rocks.

Every year toward the end of August, there is a certain feeling of regret about abandoning the house and leaving it alone for the whole winter, even though with its thick walls and nothing of value inside it is quite capable of looking after itself. Over the last few days of a vacation the washing machine is hard at work and sheets and towels are hung out to dry in the wind. When we leave the house we go out by the back door, and so don't even say goodbye to the rocks and the sea. We slink off, with a slight sense of shame, as if we were running away. One year, without any warning, my mother exclaimed: "I've said good-bye to the rocks forever!" She kept her word, for she never returned. Leaving, we carry up the bags and sacks filled with organic waste, plastic, paper, and glass, which grow a little heavier every year. One bag holds what will be needed on the ferry back to the mainland. For a while I've been in the habit of leaving behind the books I read during the summer; in the meantime I've thrown away a lot of the old and by now illegible books left there by my parents. One that has survived is a large atlas bound in red imitation leather, published in the 1960s by Selezione dal Reader's Digest, the publisher where my father worked, which is still picked up, leafed through, and appreciated today, especially by the young, more accustomed to digital and interactive maps (every home should possess an atlas, all the more so now that geography seems to be in danger of extinction). Every year I compile a meticulous list of the minor works of maintenance that ought to be done during the winter, but more often than not I lose it or cannot make head or tail of it when I find it crumpled up in Milan. I will end up making an almost identical list the following year.

At a certain point the house stopped serving as a holiday house, and instead became the expression of a part of our spirit that after dying down for much of the year germinates and blooms again in the summer. The house gives us the sensation that our life is split in two: one half urban and based on proximity, money, and compromise, and the other half wild, rough, primitive, and contrary to any mediation. The house represents this second half, and expresses the part of us which we reserve for friends who are unfazed by our eccentric and unpredictable modes of behavior. And so, progressively, the house has turned into something else; in a certain sense it has become a symbol. Even our ferry crossing to Sardinia has changed; once we set off to enjoy ourselves, now we go to reawaken something dormant. The trip has become sober and devoid of any particular excitement. The car is no longer filled with baggage, just with what is necessary. None of the entertainments offered by the shipping line tempt us, and we bring our own food and water, which we consume quietly on deck or in the cabin. Embarkation and disembarkation have become formalities, as if we were traveling by air; in the evening we disappear into the belly of the ship and reemerge the morning after.

I call my son Martino to talk about summer plans. Will they be able to come to Sardinia from London this year? Will three generations manage to overlap for a few days, or will it all be too difficult and complicated? Martino seems happier to talk of the past than of the future.

—"I remember once, I must have been eight, Nonna made a portrait of me with a red crayon in Sardinia, and I had to keep completely still. Do you have it by any chance? If not, I don't know where it could be. There was also a poem written by Nonno, but that I may have."

—"I have your portrait. In those years you used to go to Sardinia in June with your grandparents, while we stayed in Milan to work in the heat. Do you have other memories?"

—"Not many, the ones I have are all a bit blurred. I recall the trips by ship or plane, that I had to put my head down when I swam and I had to speak English, and that Nonno often had to go to hospital. I liked the dirt road at night. It seemed a remote place, a rather melancholic holiday, but not boring and anyway different from everything else."

—"But did you like the place or not?"

—"When you're little you don't have any real awareness of things like that. But it gives me pleasure to think about it today. The Sardinia of those years feels like a privilege, or rather a romantic dream, especially when viewed today from here, from London."

—"You speak of the house as if it no longer existed. Don't worry, the house is still there, and I'm taking care of it. I am even writing a book about it. A house never disappears completely, even if it's a long way from where you live."

244

Portrait of the author sitting on the Dinosaur, 1966.
Photographer Marco Scolari/Archive Sebastiano Brandolini.

The MIT Press would like to thank the anonymous peer reviewers who provided comments on drafts of this book. The generous work of academic experts is essential for establishing the authority and quality of our publications. We acknowledge with gratitude the contributions of these otherwise uncredited readers.

This book was set in Haultin by the MIT Press. Printed and bound in Canada.

Translated from the Italian by Huw Evans. Photographs, unless where credited, by Luca Casonato.

Library of Congress Cataloging-in-Publication Data

Names: Brandolini, Sebastiano, author. | Evans, Huw, translator.
Title: The house at Capo d'Orso / Sebastiano Brandolini ; translated by Huw Evans.
Description: Cambridge : The MIT Press, 2023.
Identifiers: LCCN 2022017308 | ISBN 9780262544962 (hardcover)
Subjects: LCSH: Brandolini, Sebastiano—Homes and haunts—Italy—Palau. | Vacation homes—Italy—Palau. | Palau Region (Italy)—Description and travel.
Classification: LCC NA7579.I8 B73 2023 | DDC 728.7/2094593—dc23/eng/20220902
LC record available at https://lccn.loc.gov/2022017308

10 9 8 7 6 5 4 3 2 1

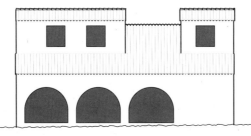